REPURPOSING YOUR LIFE

REPURPOSING YOUR LIFE

LIVING WITH INTEGRITY AND PASSION

DAVID C. COOPER

FOREWORD BY RALPH E. REED JR.

PRESS

Book Editor: Wanda Griffith
Editorial Assistant: Tammy Hatfield
Copy Editors: Esther Metaxas
Cresta Shawver
Elizabeth Hightower

Library of Congress Catalog Card Number: 2003115018
ISBN: 0-87148-465-X
Copyright © 2004 by Pathway Press
Cleveland, Tennessee 37311
All Rights Reserved
Printed in the United States of America

This book is joyfully dedicated to my mother,

Jacquelyn Peacock Cooper,

who taught me that God had a plan
and purpose for my life.

Contents

Foreword

Foreword

ℐn *Repurposing Your Life*, David Cooper has made an invaluable contribution to helping others find success and significance by reorienting their lives around their true purpose. This book is an outstanding primer of how to fulfill your destiny.

Dr. Cooper persuasively argues that it is impossible to find our destinies without understanding that we have been created by God to achieve good works for which He prepared us in advance. Unlike the platitudes and plaudits of typical self-help books, *Repurposing Your Life* asserts that faith is the foundation of the fulfilled life.

One important lesson Dr. Cooper conveys is that what you choose *not* to do is as important as deciding what to do. In the business world, this is known as "niche" marketing—finding the one thing that you do better than anyone else and doing it well. Those who try to be generalists and please everyone spread themselves too thin and do everything poorly. This is true in relation to how we manage our time, our careers, and our charitable or volunteer activities. Saying "no" to what we are not best at is the key to saying "yes" to our callings.

This book also points out that serving God and others involves more than desire. It requires discipline, focus and training. In it, David Cooper, one of the nation's most successful pastors and leaders, provides common-sense advice on how we can find that focus.

Finally, this book teaches that success and significance alone will leave you empty and without spiritual meaning. Ultimately, Cooper argues, the real purpose of success is to glorify God and to touch others with God's love and mercy. He reminds us that success in worldly terms without that objective only leads to unhappiness.

After decades of chasing materialism, professional success and a larger stock market portfolio (and finding all of these unfulfilling), there is an entire generation hungering for real purpose. Adherents and skeptics of Christianity alike will find that transcendent purpose in this important book, and in the broader spiritual movement it describes.

I have had the privilege of working with David on a personal level and know him as a friend and colleague. He puts these principles to work in his own life and ministry. The integrity and passion in this book are drawn from the lessons of the author's own enormous experiences.

Repurposing Your Life draws from the timeless principles found in the Bible and the teachings of the Christian faith. The Bible is the most valuable source of wisdom ever written. Dr. Cooper brings its ancient teachings to life with modern application. He also relates inspiring stories from giants of the Christian faith such as Billy

Graham, Martin Luther King Jr., Mother Teresa and Corrie ten Boom. Turning these pages is like having a guided tour through the "Hall of Fame of Faith." It will encourage and inspire you.

—Dr. Ralph Reed
President, Century Strategies

Introduction

Introduction

*I*f I were to ask you, "What does it take to be happy?" what would you say? Most of us think of happiness in terms of emotional security, financial stability, loving relationships, good health, enjoyable work and satisfying relationships.

But real happiness runs deeper.

Happiness comes from three inner resources. First, feelings of security. We all have the need to love and to be loved. Love makes us feel secure in the world. The deepest source of love is the love of God, which drives away all fear. When we are free from fear, we are free to live happily.

Happiness also comes from being successful. The balance of successes and failures has a lot to do with our level of personal happiness. God has a plan for each person. Knowing and doing His will is fundamental to fulfillment. We also need to use the gifts and talents God has given us. Most people work jobs that have little to do with what they are gifted to do and desire to do. They spend most of their time being employed in a field that brings them no real satisfaction. No wonder they are so unhappy.

Finally, happiness comes from finding significance. We want to know we spent our lives for a cause greater than ourselves. The older we get, the less materialistic we are and the more concerned we are about aesthetic value and spiritual issues. The ultimate joy comes from being connected with God through personal experience and living in such a way that our lives bring glory to Him and good to others.

Repurposing your life is all about getting on the right track to discover security, success and significance. You don't have to spend your life in the rat race. You can take charge of your life and discover God's dynamic purpose and plan for you.

—Dr. David C. Cooper

Chapter 1

Repurposing Your Life

I 'll never forget the day Sharon came to see me for counseling and brought me an article from the magazine *Southern Living,* entitled "Repurposing Furniture."

As she handed it to me, she said, "I ran across this article and I thought of you. Instead of refurbishing furniture, they're talking about repurposing it. Instead of just fixing it up, they're giving it a new purpose." Then she added, "That's what a lot of people need."

I completely agree. People today desperately need a sense of purpose and significance.

While imprisoned in Auschwitz, Dachau, and other German concentration camps during World War II, the renowned neurologist, Viktor Frankl, pondered the plight of those who had "enough to live by, but not enough to live for." They had the means by which to live, but their lives held no meaning.

He discovered that the last and greatest of all human

freedoms is the freedom to determine one's attitude in any given set of circumstances. The ones who survived the death camps were those who chose to find meaning even in the midst of horrible suffering.

Americans, by and large, have enough to live on but not enough to live for. We have means, but no meaning. So many people go through the routines of every week just waiting for the weekend to arrive so they can kick back and relax before they have to get back to the grind on Monday morning.

Do you have enough to live for? Are you living what Rick Warren calls "the purpose-driven life"? Or, are you just driven by an endless list of demands, enslaved to an overcrowded schedule? Do you feel that your life is out of control? Are you pushed by the pressures of life instead of being led by the Spirit?

Jesus was the most purpose-driven person who has ever lived. He had a clear sense of His identity and mission. He knew who He was and why He was here, and He made that mission unmistakably clear to those who followed Him. As we read the Gospels, we often hear Him say, "I am." "I am," He said, "the bread of life" (John 6:35, 48), "the light of the world" (8:12; 9:5), and "the resurrection and the life" (11:25).

Notice His personal mission statements:

◆ "The Son of Man did not come to be served, but to serve, and to give His life a ransom for many" (Mark 10:45, *NKJV*).

⟡ "For the Son of Man has come to seek and to save that which was lost" (Luke 19:10, *NKJV*).

⟡ "'My food,' said Jesus, 'is to do the will of him who sent me and to finish his work'" (John 4:34).

⟡ "I have come that they may have life, and have it to the full" (10:10).

Now, to the one statement Jesus made that guides us in repurposing our lives: "[Father], I have brought you glory on earth by completing the work you gave me to do" (17:4).

He offered this prayer the night of the Last Supper. His earthly ministry was over, but the Cross was before Him. The darkest night of His life was at hand. Yet, even at age 33, He could say with a deep sense of integrity that He had finished the work God had given Him. Because of that, He knew He had achieved the ultimate purpose of life—bringing glory to God.

The Westminster Larger Catechism poses the question: "What is the chief and highest end of man?" Answer: "Man's chief and highest end is to glorify God, and fully to enjoy him forever."

Let's be honest. We've all gotten away from this truth at some time or another. Things started out well, but then came unraveled. When this happens, we need to repurpose our lives.

A close friend shared the following story with me.

A San Diego patrolman pulled over a car and told the

driver that because he was wearing his seat belt, he had just won $5,000 in a statewide safety competition.

"What are you going to do with the money?" the officer asked.

"I guess I'll go to driving school and get my license," the man answered.

"Don't listen to him," said the woman in the passenger seat. "He's a smart aleck when he's been drinking."

This woke up the guy in the back seat, who saw the cop and shouted, "I knew we wouldn't get far in a stolen car."

Then there was knock from the trunk and voice asked in Spanish, "Are we over the border yet?"

Now that's going from bad to worse!

Jesus' simple prayer in John 17:4 gives us three cues to repurposing our lives and getting back on track.

You Have a Calling From God

What would you think if I told you that God has a plan for you? The fact is, He does! God's plan for us involves two principles. First, God designed each of us to fulfill a specific purpose, and we only find significance when we live out His plan. Second, God expects us to develop our gifts and talents in order to reach our potential. We have a part to play.

Jesus knew He had a calling from God at a very young age. By the age of 12, He was discussing matters of religion with the teachers of the law. "I must be about My

Father's business," He said to His parents when they came
to get Him at the Temple (Luke 2:49, *NKJV*).

As we go about the routines of daily living, we too
should be about the Father's business. Ministry is not
something we do when life stops and we have time. It's
what we do all the time. It
is the thread that weaves
every activity and rela-
tionship together. Life is a

> Ministry is the thread that weaves every activity and relationship together.

single-minded pursuit to know and to do the will of God.
Your work is your calling, and your career is your divine
vocation. Let the light of Christ shine through you right
where God has placed you.

You are not here by accident; God ordained your existence. The Old Testament prophet Jeremiah learned this
valuable lesson when God spoke to him: "Then the word
of the Lord came to me, saying, 'Before I formed you in
the womb I knew you; Before you were born I sanctified
you; I ordained you a prophet to the nations'" (Jeremiah
1:4, 5, *NKJV*). The word Jeremiah used for *knew* actually could mean "chose." God told Jeremiah that He chose
him before he was formed in his mother's womb. The
same is true for you!

⬦ You are God's masterpiece!

⬦ You have eyes that can distinguish approximately
8 million colors.

⬦ You have ears consisting of 20,000 hairs discern-
ing 300,000 tones.

- You have a circulatory system that is 60-100 miles long.

- Your heart pumps 5 quarts of blood per minute, which equals 2,000 gallons per day.

- You produce 1 billion red blood cells every day.

- You develop 200 miles of capillaries for every one pound of body fat.

- You have a muscular system consisting of 600 muscles that could lift 25 tons if used together.

- You have a nervous system consisting of 10 million nerves.

- You have 1,300 nerve endings on every square inch of fingertip that send touch sensations to the brain at the rate of 350 feet per second.

- You have a skeletal structure consisting of 206 bones. One square inch of bone can withstand a two-ton force!

- You have a digestive tract that is 30 feet long.

- You have lungs that contain 600 million air sacs and breathe 2,400 gallons of air daily. The surface area of the lungs is 1,000 square feet, which is 20 times greater than the surface area of the skin on your body.

◆ You have skin containing 19 million cells, 625 sweat glands, 65 hairs, 19 feet of blood vessels and 19,000 sensory cells on each square inch! Microscopic animals live on its surface—the human skin is infested with mites. (This is getting gross, but it's going somewhere.) The body constantly sheds skin cells and replaces them with new ones, so much so that 75 percent of dust in the average house is made up of dead skin cells.

◆ You have a stomach with acid powerful enough to dissolve a razor blade. To keep from digesting itself, the stomach produces a new lining every 3 days.

◆ You have a brain weighing about 3 pounds and containing some 100 billion neurons. Each neuron is like a small computer. The brain has more than 100,000 chemical reactions occurring every second. Nerve cells send impulses to the body at the rate of 200 miles per second. The brain stores 10-15 trillion memories in a lifetime.

Considering the fantastic human body, the psalmist exclaimed, "I am fearfully and wonderfully made; marvelous are Your works" (Psalm 139:14, *NKJV*).

You Are to Do Only the Work God Has Given You to Do

Jesus prayed, "I have finished the work which *You have given Me to do*" (John 17:4, *NKJV*, emphasis added). We need to focus on the work God has given us to do, not the work everybody else tries to give us to do!

When Jesus said He finished the work, not everyone had been saved or healed. Not everyone believed in Him. The kingdom of God had not overtaken the kingdoms of this world. How could Jesus say He had finished anything? Well, He qualified exactly what it was He had finished—the work God gave Him to do.

What was His work? First, His work was to train the Twelve to carry on His ministry after His resurrection and to inaugurate the coming of the kingdom of God. Second, His work was to go to the Cross and pay the penalty for our sins, so that we might be forgiven and have eternal life.

The goal of life is to finish the unique work God has given each one of us to do. Herein lies the secret to both success and significance. People will try to give you all kinds of work to do throughout your life. If you're not careful, you will be driven by an over-committed schedule. The question is, has God called you to do this work?

Jesus spoke often of work. People can see our "good works" and glorify God (Matthew 5:16). Jesus said we need to work while we have the time because "the night is coming when no one can work" (John 9:4). He declared that finishing the work God gave Him to do provided a sense of satisfaction in life (John 4:34).

In the movie comedy, *The Blues Brothers,* Jake says to Elwood, "We're on a mission from God." The fact is, we all are!

Life itself is a mission from God. So, I ask you again,

what work has God given you to do? Have you discovered it? Are you focusing your time, energy and resources
on that work? Or are you distracted from your real mission because of all the work others have given you to do?
It's time to repurpose your life and focus on the work God
has given you to do.

I think the Messiah was the only person of His time
who never struggled with a messianic complex. He had
no delusions of grandeur. He was never in a hurry, but He
maintained a clear sense of mission. He stuck to His plan
without getting distracted, going about His work in a
calm, peaceful manner. He kept His balance.

Time is of the essence. God gave us the system of time
at the dawn of creation **We need to use time wisely**
as a way of organizing **and move forward with our**
life. We need to use **lives by focusing only on**
time wisely and move **what God has given us to do.**
forward with our lives
by focusing only on what God has given us to do.

Jesus began this great prayer of John 17 with the
words: "Father, the time has come" (v. 1). Speaking of
His passion on the cross, Jesus had a clear sense of time.

When you are clear as to what God wants you to do,
you also become clear as to what God does *not* want you
to do. Knowing what not to do in life is as important as
knowing what to do. We waste so much precious time
doing things we don't need to be doing.

There's an interesting statement about King David
recorded in Acts 13:22: "He will do everything [God

wants] him to do"—but not necessarily everything other people wanted David to do.

What would you do if you suddenly found $86,000 invested in your bank account? How would you use it? Every day God deposits into our lives 86,000 seconds, which is 1,440 minutes, or 24 hours. Time can be invested, wasted, used wisely or neglected, but it cannot be saved. We are to make "the most of every opportunity" (Ephesians 5:16).

We battle what has been called "the tyranny of the urgent." As Carl Jung wrote, "Hurry is not of the devil; hurry is the devil."

Every day I ask myself, "What definitely has to get done today?" Then I organize my day around the important, so I cannot be distracted by the urgent.

Identify the five most important people in your life, the five most important long-range goals, and the five most important aspects of your career. Keep your time invested in the important people and goals, and you will avoid the trap of the tyranny of the urgent.

As World War II was drawing to a close, C.S. Lewis, literature professor at Magdalen College in Oxford, England, lectured a group of his students. He paused and asked the class, "How can you go to college and study literature when London is under siege?"

Then he answered his own question. "We're always under siege. The real question is: Will you spend your life dealing with the immediate or the eternal?"

Jesus sought only to bring glory to God—that was His overarching purpose. How different our Day Timers and Palm Pilots would look if we only did those things and got involved in those projects that would bring glory to God.

That's exactly how you repurpose your life.

Be a Finisher, Not Just a Starter

Jesus lived His life in such a way that He could honestly say, "I have completed the work." Finishing is a vital principle in life.

When my son was about 5, we put him in a community soccer league. It was organized chaos on the field, and he wanted to quit because he didn't enjoy it. I said, "You have to finish what you started, but if you don't want to play after this season, that will be OK." The point is, it's

> It's OK to change direction in life, but it's not OK to quit. Quitting weakens character, while finishing builds it.

OK to change direction in life, but it's not OK to quit. Quitting weakens character, while finishing builds it.

God "finished" the work of Creation (Genesis 2:1, *NKJV*). Jesus shouted from the cross in triumph, "It is finished" (John 19:30, *NKJV*). God promises to finish the work of grace He started in us (Philippians 1:6). The apostle Paul faced martyrdom saying, "I have finished the race" (2 Timothy 4:7, *NKJV*). The world is full of starters but lacking in finishers.

A famous painting from World War I shows an engineer

repairing a field telephone line. He had just completed the line so that an essential message could be delivered when he was shot. The painting shows him in the moment of death. Beneath it is one word, "Through!"

You need two things to be a finisher. First, like Jesus, stay focused on your goals. Luke writes, "Jesus resolutely set out for Jerusalem" (Luke 9:51). Translated literally, He "set his face like a flint."

Several years ago I had the opportunity of having dinner with Sir Roger Bannister as a part of the Cobb County 10K Race. Bannister was the first person to break the four-minute mile, representing the British Amateur Athletic Association at an Oxford meet in 1954. His performance is known as "The Miracle Mile."

During that famous race, he was running closely with Australian John Landy, who was about two strides ahead. Then, when Landy turned and looked over his left shoulder, Bannister shot past him in that split second on the right hand side and won the race by a couple of yards. A lapse of concentration can cost a great deal.

The second quality needed to be a finisher is to develop a marathon mentality. Life is a marathon, not a sprint. You have to find your own pace and stick to it. Those who press on will finish. Success and accomplishment belong to those who hang in there when others quit.

Jesus' joy was to finish the work God had given Him to do. He is "the author *and finisher* of our faith" (Hebrews 12:2, *NKJV*, emphasis added). Let us fix our eyes on Him as we run the race of life. He is our example of endurance in the face of hardship. He is our source of strength. Let us find joy in finishing the work He has given each of us to do.

His work was finished that we might have eternal life. "This is eternal life," He prayed to the Father, "that they may know You, the only true God, and Jesus Christ whom You have sent" (John 17:3, *NKJV*). Eternal life means enjoying the highest quality of life today, as well as spending eternity in heaven.

I pause here to ask if you have accepted the finished work of Jesus for your salvation. If not, receive Him today as your Savior. Repurposing your life begins with placing Christ at the center of your life. "Believe on the Lord Jesus Christ, and you will be saved" (Acts 16:31, *NKJV*).

Chapter 2

Getting Past Your Past

Getting Past Your Past

Have you ever wished your life had a rewind button so you could travel back in time? You could relive a great moment of your life or do something differently, like correct a mistake you made with your kids. You could even undo something you regret and make things right.

I certainly wish life came with a rewind button but, unfortunately, it doesn't. The main business of life is to make the most of today.

Missed opportunities, secret sins and irreversible decisions can a form a prison, locking us out of the present. We can romanticize the past and remember the glory of days gone by—like a "40-something" woman who cherishes her memories of being on the high school homecoming court.

William Wordsworth wrote, "The child is father of the man." We are definitely influenced by the past, but we don't have to get stuck in it. The past should be an asset, not a liability.

Some people drag the past around like Linus drags his blanket in Charles Schulz's cartoon strip *Peanuts*. They are always dealing with the past in one way or another. They are preoccupied with such ideas as getting over the past, forgetting the past, working through the past and so forth.

The problem is, every minute spent working on the past is another minute lost to the present. Of course, there are legitimate times to deal with past issues, but it should be done intentionally and with the goal of moving past the past. The only way your past can be an asset to you is if you use it as a teacher—a springboard to launch you into the future.

> Every minute spent working on the past is another minute lost to the present.

Let's challenge the notion of "working through" the past. We tend to make a bigger deal about the influence of the past than is justified. The reason you think, feel or act a certain way is not always due to the past.

According to modern-day logic, you have to explore your past to understand yourself. To change yourself, you have to resolve the past, often through therapy or inner healing, in order to move on in life. This whole line of thinking leads us down the path of blaming the past instead of taking charge of the present.

There's nothing wrong with analyzing the past, and it may be beneficial up to a point, but it won't change the present. Action is required. Understanding everything about your past wouldn't change the present. You have to set goals and implement a plan of action to change your life.

Mark this down: *Understanding your past will not change the present.*

The past no longer exists. You can't undo it, change it or go back and relive it. The past is what it is—the past.

"What can I do with the past?" you may ask.

You can . . .

- Be thankful for the past.

- Regret the past.

- Grieve over the past.

- Live in the past.

- Learn from the past.

- Romanticize the past.

- Forget the past.

- Blame the past.

- Celebrate the past.

- *But you can't change the past.*

Since you can change only the present, focus your energy on the here and now. You don't have the luxury of going back and starting over and getting it right this time. Your life, like mine, is a mixture of good and bad experiences, successes and failures, pain and pleasure. Your negative experiences are just as important as the positive experiences in the equation of who you are. Don't be

> Your negative experiences are just as important as the positive experiences in the equation of who you are.

ashamed of your past, or embarrassed by your past, or in denial of your past. Make it your ally, instead of your adversary, by learning from it. Yesterday's mistakes can make you a better person today if you learn from them.

Don't Get Over It, Get on With It!

We waste valuable time regretting the past and fretting the future. Life is right now, not yesterday and not tomorrow. Now! The key to getting past your past is to make the most of the moment.

Latch on to this truth: *The past is resolved when the present is fulfilled.*

When you are happy, you don't waste time analyzing your past. You're too busy enjoying life. It's only when life comes to a grinding halt that you get preoccupied with the past. It is time for you to stop asking, *How can I get over my past?* and start asking, *How can I get on with my life?*

My phone rang late one night during the Christmas season. The lady on the other end of the line was distraught. Her husband had passed away about six months earlier. Although we had talked on a several occasions as I tried to help her work through the grieving process, she continued to be stuck in her bereavement and depression.

"How can I ever get over Ray's death?" she cried. "I'm so alone. I've got nothing left to live for."

Suddenly, a thought popped into my head and I blurted out, *"Don't get over it, get on with it!"*

My words hit her like a ton of bricks. She regained her composure. There was an awkward moment of silence. Then she asked, "What do you mean—get on with it?"

I thought to myself, "What do I mean?"

I told her she would always love her husband, and she would always miss him. No one could take away the pain and loss she felt. "Your pain," I said, "is the measure of your love. Stop trying to get over Ray's death. There are some things in life we never get over, and this is one of them, but you can get on with it. Keep your pain tucked away in your heart. Treasure your memories of Ray forever. But begin to live the rest of your life in spite of your pain."

After our conversation, and several subsequent ones, she began to understand the principle: *Don't get over it, get on with!* She started to dream again. She thought about . . .

- ◆ Places to travel

- ◆ Career opportunities

- ◆ New skills to develop

- ◆ Educational challenges

♦ Volunteer opportunities

♦ Charitable causes

♦ A new place to live.

She rose to meet the challenge of getting on with life even when it hurts. It may shock you to hear me say this, but there are some things you'll experience that are so painful you'll never get over them. The good news is you don't have to—you can always get on with it even when you can't get over it.

Let me show you this powerful truth as explained in Scripture:

> But one thing I do: Forgetting what is behind and straining toward what is ahead, I press on toward the goal to win the prize for which God has called me heavenward in Christ Jesus (Philippians 3:13, 14).

When the Israelites were trapped in the desert after they had been delivered from Egypt, they were in serious trouble. Pharaoh's army pursued them from behind. The Red Sea was in front. The situation looked hopeless. They were terrified and complained to Moses, "Let's go back to Egypt!"

But Moses prayed, and God answered him: "Then the Lord said to Moses, 'Why are you crying out to me? Tell the Israelites to move on'" (Exodus 14:15).

That's exactly what God says when we're stuck in the past and paralyzed by fear, resentment, failure, tragedy or disappointment: *Move on!*

The Fine Art of Forgetting

Getting on with life begins by putting the past into perspective. Paul tells us that he learned to forget the things that are behind. Our problem is that we tend to remember the things we should forget and forget the things we should remember. As Italo Svevo once said, "There are three things I

> Getting on with life begins by putting the past into perspective.

always forget: Names, faces—and the third I can't remember."

1. *Forget the accomplishments of the past.* Don't allow your life to become a museum. Don't waste time reliving the glory of the past by polishing trophies and displaying blue ribbon awards. While your accomplishments are great and should be celebrated, your greatest achievements are yet ahead.

Someone asked Rembrandt, "Of all your paintings, which one is the greatest?"

He said, "I don't know. I haven't painted it yet."

One day Charles Schwab received a telegram from one of his salesmen telling him he had, the day before, sold the largest single order for steel in the history of the company. Mr. Schwab wired back, "That's wonderful. What have you done *today?*"

2. *Forget the analysis of the past.* Analysis tends toward passivity, or what E. Stanley Jones called "the paralysis of analysis." While it is normal to wonder why certain things happen, or why things turned out the way they did, all our speculations are just that—*speculations!*

Who can say for sure why things happen? Job's com-
forters thought they knew all the answers after they ana-
lyzed Job's sufferings. In the end, God told them they were
all wrong (Job 42:7-9).

Here's an axiom to help you take charge of your life:
Don't ask why, ask what. Focus your energies on setting
goals and solving problems instead of mulling over the
past. *What* you can do today is more important than understanding *why*
things happened yesterday.

> Focus your energies on setting goals and solving problems instead of mulling over the past.

3. *Forget the agonies of the past.* First, there is the
agony of our sins. We vowed to say no to sin, only to say
yes. We determined to stand firm against temptation, only
to collapse under the pressure. We resolved to believe,
only to end up doubting.

When we fail, the most difficult task is to forgive ourselves. It's fairly easy to receive forgiveness from God,
but forgiving ourselves is tough. To get on with life, you
have to forgive yourself. Besides, if God forgives you,
how can you not forgive yourself? Are you greater than
God?

Pray this prayer of the psalmist if you are stuck in guilt:

> Have mercy on me, O God, according to your unfailing
> love; according to your great compassion blot out my
> transgressions. Wash away all my iniquity and cleanse
> me from my sin. . . . Cleanse me with hyssop, and I will
> be clean; wash me, and I will be whiter than snow. . . .

Create in me a pure heart, O God, and renew a steadfast spirit within me. Do not cast me from your presence or take your Holy Spirit from me. Restore to me the joy of your salvation and grant me a willing spirit, to sustain me. Then I will teach transgressors your ways, and sinners will turn back to you. . . . The sacrifices of God are a broken spirit; a broken and contrite heart, O God, you will not despise (Psalm 51:1, 2, 7, 10-13, 17).

God says, "Your sins are forgiven!" Now, forgive yourself.

4. *Forget the agony of suffering.* Suffering is no respecter of persons. It comes in many forms. Emotional scars. Crushing disappointments. Lost opportunities. Personal losses. Family tragedies. Ruined relationships. Shattered hopes.

The most common form of baggage from the past is resentment. "See to it that no one misses the grace of God and that no bitter root grows up to cause trouble and defile many" (Hebrews 12:15).

Release your resentments and forgive those who have wronged you. Martin Luther said, "My soul is too glad and too great to be at heart the enemy of any man." God

> The most common form of baggage from the past is resentment.

has a promise for you: "Forget the former things; do not dwell on the past. See, I am doing a new thing! Now it springs up; do you not perceive it? I am making a way in the desert and streams in the wasteland" (Isaiah 43:18, 19).

The story is told of two Buddhist monks walking

together in a thunderstorm. They came to a swollen stream. A beautiful young Japanese woman in a kimono stood there wanting to cross to the other side but afraid of the currents.

One of the monks said, "Can I help you?"

"I need to cross this stream," replied the woman.

The monk picked her up, put her on his shoulders, carried her through the swirling waters, and put her down on the other side. He and his companion then went on to the monastery.

That night his companion said to him, "I have a bone to pick with you. As Buddhist monks, we have taken vows not to look on a woman, much less touch her body. Back there by the river you did both."

"My brother," answered the other monk, "I put that woman down on the other side of the river. You're still carrying her in your mind."

"E" Is for Effort

When we learn to forget, we're ready to make progress. Paul says he strains for what lies ahead (Philippians 3:13). The word *strain* is an athletic term and could describe an Olympic runner stretching out with all his energy to cross the finish line and win first place. With an all-consuming focus on the prize, the runner lunges forward, stretching out his body to cross the finish line with all the energy he can muster.

Take a look at your own life. What do you see ahead

for you? Do you have a dream for your life? What do you want to accomplish? Now is the time to get a clear sense of the direction of your life and go for it with all your might. As Theodore Roosevelt said, "If you are not actively pursuing the person you want to be, you are pursuing the person you don't want to be."

The apostle Paul had a sense of destiny. "I press on to take hold of that for which Christ Jesus took hold of me" (Philippians 3:12). He believed Jesus had taken hold of his life on the Damascus Road for a particular purpose.

Christ intends every person to attain some higher, spiritual purpose. Jesus Christ took hold of you when you came to know Him. He seized possession of your life that He might use you as an instrument of His praise. You have eternal significance and a divine destiny. Now go for it!

The will of God does not come to pass passively. We must, in Jesus' words, take the kingdom by force (Matthew 11:12). Many people are too passive in their pursuits. Some view the blessings of God as some kind of divine luck, arbitrarily making some people successful and other mediocre.

> God's blessings are not random. They follow faith, obedience and perseverance.

God's blessings are not random. They follow faith, obedience and perseverance.

Stay off the path of least resistance. I once read about how the road system came to be developed in Boston. If you were to visit Boston and study the road system, you might conclude there was no master design at all to the roads. They wind around with little rhyme or reason in their layout, because early roads were developed along cow paths.

Cows form paths by following the path of least resistance. When cows walk up hills they don't say, "Here's a hill. Let's navigate the best path possible." No, they simply follow the path of least resistance, stepping around the next rock or steep grade. When they return to the same area, they simply follow the previous course, eventually beating down the grass and forming a path.

Human nature also tends to follow the path of least resistance. However, the good life belongs to those who take the road not taken, the road of diligence, vision and commitment.

America is plagued by those who take the path of least resistance. Look at education and what has been called the "dumbing-down" of America. Instead of providing higher quality education, we lower the academic standards so everyone can be an A student.

Some athletic programs have even eliminated the concept of losing in order that everyone can be a winner, as if losing would damage a child's psyche. Rather, losing is fundamental in the development of the determination and perseverance needed for achieving success. Everyone should experience the pain of losing so they can appreciate the joy of victory. The treacherous climb to the top of the mountain, the long journey through the hot desert sands and the hard knocks experienced through trial and error are necessary ingredients in reaching our highest potential.

The word is *strain*. Oswald Chambers, in his classic devotional *My Utmost for His Highest,* writes: "God does not give us overcoming life. He gives us life as we overcome. The strain is the strength. If there is no strain, there is no strength. Are you asking God to give you life and liberty and joy? He cannot, unless you are willing to accept the strain."

> The treacherous climb to the top of the mountain, the long journey through the hot desert sands and the hard knocks experienced through trial and error are necessary ingredients in reaching our highest potential.

No pain, no gain. Late one night, Jesus' disciples were caught in a ferocious storm on the Sea of Galilee. Jesus "saw the disciples straining at the oars, because the wind was against them" (Mark 6:48). That's a perfect picture of life. The winds of change, loss, failure, adversity, disappointment and fear blow hard against us. The only way we can make it to the desired destination is to strain at the oars.

- Strain to reach your goals.
- Strain to have a good marriage.
- Strain to build a happy home.
- Strain to get your education.
- Strain to achieve financial success.

◆ Strain to release your potential.

◆ Strain for what lies ahead.

God knows how much we can handle.

No temptation has seized you except what is common to man. And God is faithful; he will not let you be tempted beyond what you can bear. But when you are tempted, he will also provide a way out so that you can stand up under it (1 Corinthians 10:13).

I can identify with Mother Teresa, who said, "I know God will not give me anything I can't handle. I just wish He didn't trust me so much."

Repurposing your life takes an action plan with clearly defined goals.

You need goals to go along with your oars. Without goals, you'll spend your time straining but not accomplishing anything. Repurposing your life takes an action plan with clearly defined goals. J.C. Penney said, "Give me a stock clerk with a goal and I'll give you a man who will make history. Give me a man with no goals and I'll give you a stock clerk."

Look Ahead, Not Behind

Where you're going is more important that where you've been. Lot's wife was guilty of looking back. You too may be looking back to your past and missing out on the moment. Instead, look ahead to your future.

When Israel faced the challenges of the wilderness

they kept looking back to the comforts of Egypt, as if being a slave in Egypt were a comfortable life! Their reward for looking back was not a first class ticket to Egypt, but 40 years of wandering in the desert. Looking back will have the same effect in your life. You will miss your Promised Land if you don't learn to look ahead instead of behind.

U.S. diplomat and former Hollywood child star Shirley Temple Black told a story about her husband, Charles, and his mother. When he was a boy, he asked his mother what the happiest moment of her life was.

"This moment—right now," she responded.

"But what about all the other happy moments in your life?" he said. "What about when you were married?"

She answered, "My happiest moment then was then, my happiest moment now is now. You can only really live in the moment you're in. So, to me that's always the happiest moment."

I had the privilege of hearing Dr. Condoleeza Rice, national security advisor, speak at the 2003 National Prayer Breakfast in Washington D.C. She shared her testimony of how, after growing up as a pastor's daughter, she strayed from her Christian upbringing, and later found her way back.

As a young adult, she got out of the habit of going to church. One Sunday morning, while shopping at the Lucky Grocery Store when she should have been in church, she ran into a man who told her he was shopping for a church picnic that afternoon. He asked if she played the piano, because they needed a pianist at their church. She told him she was actually trained in classical piano.

She was shocked how far God's hand could reach— all the way into the Lucky Grocery Store. She started playing piano for this Baptist church, but she had a hard time with their music, having been raised Presbyterian. She was trained classically, but they were singing gospel music. The pastor would start singing in a key that did- n't exist, and the musicians had to follow along.

She called her mother, who also played piano for a church, and asked, "What should I do to keep up with them when I can't find the key they are singing in?" Her mother gave her great advice: "Just play in the key of C, and they'll come back to you."

> God always plays in C, and even though we may drift from Him, we will always find our way back.

Dr. Rice then added, "God always plays in C, and even though we may drift from Him, we will always find our way back."

Repurposing your life begins with finding your way back to Him.

Chapter 3

Releasing Your Resentments

ome people never get on with life because they carry too much baggage from the past—*unfinished business*. It's hard enough to deal with today's challenges without struggling with past issues as well. Repurposing your life requires resolving unfinished business, the most common type of which is resentment.

Resentment means "harboring a grudge, being unwilling to forgive, or wishing harm or ill will to another as a result of real or imagined injury." The word *resentment* literally means "to feel again." A person filled with resentment clings tightly to the past, reliving hurts, disappointments and injustices over and over until only a callused, bitter and guarded person remains and says to the world, "I'll never let you hurt me again!"

Have you ever found yourself saying, "I have a right to be resentful"? That's one of the most self-defeating messages you can send. The truth is, we don't have the right to be resentful. Resentment imprisons both the person who is resentful and the person he or she resents.

A Lesson From the Past

One person whose circumstances could have easily led to resentment was Joseph, whose story is told in Genesis. He had a long list of good reasons why he could have been resentful. His brothers were so jealous of him, they sold him to Ishmaelite merchants who eventually took him to Egypt and sold him as a slave to a man named Potiphar. While Joseph was working for Potiphar, Potiphar's wife tried to seduce Joseph. When he resisted her advances, she was so infuriated she accused him of attempted rape. Potiphar, whom Joseph had served faithfully, refused to hear Joseph's side of the story and condemned him to prison.

While in prison, Joseph interpreted the dream of Pharaoh's cupbearer. The cupbearer promised to help Joseph get out of prison after his own release. He soon was released from prison just as Joseph predicted, but he forgot about Joseph, leaving him incarcerated.

Joseph could have resented God. After all, God gave him the dream that he would rule over his family. His brothers would have never been jealous of him had it not been for that dream. He could have easily told himself it was all God's fault that his life had ended up the way it had. However, instead of choosing resentment, Joseph chose to take the moral high ground. He transcended his feelings of resentment through the power of forgiveness.

After 12 years in prison and his miraculous exaltation to second in command to Pharaoh, Joseph was reconciled to his brothers. Genesis 45 recounts that touching scene when he revealed his identity to his brothers. They had not seen Joseph since they had sold him into slavery. Naturally, they had assumed he was dead. They went to Egypt to get food because there was a famine in Canaan, and there was enough grain stored in Egypt to provide for the region. They had no idea that Joseph served as second in command to Pharaoh and, although they spoke with him about getting food and supplies to take back to their home, they did not realize they were talking to their own brother. Apparently, he had become Egyptian in dress and manner.

Finally, Joseph could no longer hold back his emotions. He revealed his identity to his brothers and all seemed well. But when their father died, the brothers became worried that Joseph would finally seek revenge.

When Joseph's brothers saw that their father was dead, they said, "What if Joseph holds a grudge against us and pays us back for all the wrongs we did to him?" So they sent word to Joseph, saying, "Your father left these instructions before he died: 'This is what you are to say to Joseph: "I ask you to forgive your brothers the sins and the wrongs they committed in treating you so badly." ' Now please forgive the sins of the servants of the God of your father." When their message came to him, Joseph wept. His brothers then came and threw themselves down before him. "We are your slaves," they said. But Joseph said to them, "Don't be afraid. Am I in the place of God? You intended to harm me, but God intended it for good to accomplish what is now being done, the saving of many lives. So then, don't be afraid. I will provide for you and your children." And he reassured them and spoke kindly to them (Genesis 50:15-21).

Face Your Feelings

We need to confront feelings of resentment. Leonardo da Vinci experienced a sharp disagreement with a fellow painter just before he began his work on "The Last Supper." He chose to paint the face of that man as the face of Judas Iscariot as a way of expressing his resentment. But as he later prepared to paint the face of Jesus, he felt no inspiration.

Finally, he owned up to his resentment and confessed it to God. He then repainted the face of Judas, and the inspiration came for him to paint the majestic portrait of the Son of God. The painting was completed. We can't expect God to paint the image of Christ in us while we paint others with the colors of resentment.

> We can't expect God to paint the image of Christ in us while we paint others with the colors of resentment.

One of the worst things a person can do is to deny and repress resentment. Repressed feelings eventually find a way of getting out. Dreams serve as a release mechanism for painful and disturbing memories locked up in the unconscious mind. At times we're even unconsciously motivated by hidden fears and resentments.

Sigmund Freud compared the human mind to an iceberg. The smallest portion, standing above the surface of the water, is the conscious mind. The larger portion, beneath the surface of the water, is the unconscious mind.

If I asked you, "What is two plus two?" you would immediately answer, "Four." If I asked you to tell me your name, your address, or what you do for a living, you could readily tell me. And there are thousands of other pieces of data you can retrieve from your memory by a simple act of your will. That's the conscious mind at work. But if I asked you to tell me about your second birthday, you probably couldn't do it. The memory is physiologically recorded by the brain, but you can't retrieve the information at will.

We tend to repress painful memories and traumatic experiences in the unconscious mind. We repress those memories by refusing to deal with issues or by denying that the events ever happened. But the feelings and memories lie hidden beneath the surface, continuing to affect the way we think, feel and relate to others.

Repression has drastic consequences. Repressed emotions can result in physical symptoms called psychosomatic illnesses. Our behavior is often motivated by the unconscious mind. Repressed issues and feelings related to the past keep us from living fully in the present.

The Scripture is clear on this point of unfinished business: "See to it that no one misses the grace of God and that no bitter root grows up to cause trouble and defile many" (Hebrews 12:15). The first step in dealing with resentment is to uproot all bitterness. Repressed feelings of resentment trouble and destroy relationships, but when we release our resentments, we discover the pathway to freedom.

Amazing Grace

This freedom is due to the amazing power of God's grace in our hearts. Look again at the verse above: "See to it that no one misses the grace of God." If we miss out on grace, God's unconditional love and mercy for us, we will be trapped by resentments.

> **If we miss out on grace, God's unconditional love and mercy for us, we will be trapped by resentments.**

"God has poured out his love into our hearts by the Holy Spirit, whom he has given us" (Romans 5:5). When the Spirit of God empowers us, we can and will forgive as He has forgiven us. Forgiveness leads to emotional freedom.

In 1946, Czeslaw Godlewski was a member of a young gang that roamed and sacked the German countryside. On an isolated farm, they gunned down ten members of the Wilhelm Hamelmann family. Nine of the victims died, but Hamelmann himself survived his four bullet wounds. After Godlewski completed a 20-year prison term for his crimes, the state would not release him because he had nowhere to go. When Hamelmann learned of the situation, he asked the authorities to release Godlewski to his custody. He wrote in his request: "Messiah died for my sins and forgave me. Should I not then forgive this man?" [1]

E. Stanley Jones talks about three levels of possible response to the wrongs done to us. We can return evil for evil—that's human. We can return evil for good—that's demonic. Or, we can return good for evil—that's divine. "Do not be overcome by evil, but overcome evil with good" (Romans 12:21).

James Hewett tells the following story about radical forgiveness. During the Korean War, a South Korean Christian, a civilian, was arrested by the Communists and ordered shot. But when the young Communist leader learned that the prisoner had been in charge of an orphanage caring for small children, he decided to spare the man and execute his 19-year-old son instead. They shot the boy in the presence of his father.

Later the fortunes of war changed, and the young Communist leader was captured by the United Nations forces, tried for war crimes and condemned to die. Before the sentence was carried out, the Christian whose boy had been killed pleaded for the life of the young officer. He said the man was young, acted under orders and did not really know what he was doing. "Give him to me," he pleaded, "and I will train him how to live."

The United Nations granted the request and the father

took the murderer of his own son into his home. Later, that young man became a Christian pastor. No wonder John Newton, the composer of the beloved hymn, called it "*Amazing Grace*"!

Nearly everyone has heard the name of Corrie ten Boom. She and her sister, Betsie, were imprisoned in the Nazi prison camp Ravensbruck during World War II. They suffered abuse, torture and starvation. Betsie died in the camp.

After the war, Corrie traveled, preaching the gospel. She dreaded the day she might run into one of the Nazi soldiers who had guarded them at Ravensbruck. After a speaking engagement in Munich, a strangely familiar man greeted her. Suddenly she realized he was a soldier who had guarded Betsie and her. A rush of anger and resentment welled up inside her, even though she thought those feelings had been resolved.

What would she do? How would she respond?

Quietly she prayed, "Oh God, help me forgive this man."

The man said, "Fraulein, what you said tonight is true. God does forgive and cleanse us of our sins. But will you forgive me?"

Corrie ten Boom later said, "As I grabbed his hand, an incredible thing took place. The current started in my shoulder, raced down my arm and sprang into our joined hands. And then this healing warmth seemed to flood my whole being, literally bringing tears to my eyes. 'I forgive you, brother! With all my heart.'"

An Unaffordable Luxury

A man telephoned an exquisite restaurant. He asked the maitre'd, "What is the price range of your meals?" The maitre'd responded, "Believe me, if you have to ask, you can't afford it."

Unforgiveness is a luxury we can't afford; it eats away at relationships like a cancer. Jesus told us in no uncertain terms to get rid of resentments. In the center of the Lord's Prayer stands the petition: "Forgive us our debts, as we also have forgiven our debtors" (Matthew 6:12).

> Unforgiveness is a luxury we can't afford; it eats away at relationships like a cancer.

Forgiveness is not a feeling. You may forgive someone and still have feelings of hurt and disappointment.

Forgiveness is not an event. It's a process. Jesus told us to forgive people "seventy times seven" (Matthew 18:22, *NKJV*). You may have to remind yourself every day that you have forgiven someone when feelings of resentment resurface.

Forgiveness is not forgetting. Even though our brains store all memories, we need to forget the hurt, pain or injustice done against us. Forgiveness does not provide amnesia. We forget in the sense that we release any grudges against those who hurt us.

Forgiveness is not a miracle. True, God will help you forgive, but *you* must do the forgiving. You can't ask God to miraculously make all the hurt feelings disappear. Forgiveness is not a matter of miracles but of maturity.

Forgiveness is not reconciliation. You may forgive someone but not be reconciled to him. Unlike reconciliation, forgiveness only takes one person. Just because you forgive someone doesn't mean he or she will necessarily accept your forgiveness or respond to your gestures of grace. Perhaps they will accept their responsibility and reconciliation will occur, but the truth is, not all forgiveness results in reconciliation. Jesus forgave the whole world its sins when He died on the cross. "Father, forgive them," he prayed (Luke 23:34). But not everyone has received His forgiveness or become reconciled to God.

Forgiveness is not submission to abuse or negligence in any relationship. While we are commanded by God to forgive everyone, we are not expected to remain in destructive relationships. Love sets boundaries.

So, what is forgiveness? Forgiveness is a powerful spiritual principle and means . . .

- ◆ to cancel the debt

- ◆ to forget the matter

- ◆ to release the right to resentment

- ◆ to forfeit the privilege of revenge

- ◆ to give up any grudge

- ◆ to remove all guilt

- ◆ to pardon all sin.

Take a moment and read that list again. Forgiveness essentially means to release. When you forgive others, you release them from any debt, from any need to apologize, from any need to make things right, from any obligation whatsoever. Forgiveness is basically a financial term meaning "to cancel the debt." (Don't you wish your credit card company understood the meaning of the word forgiveness?)

We should live every day as if it were Jubilee. That was the Jewish year of canceling debts and returning all properties to the original owners. The Year of Jubilee kept the economy from experiencing a depression and gave every person and family the opportunity to start over

> When you forgive others, you release them from any debt, from any need to apologize, from any need to make things right, from any obligation whatsoever.

financially. We should do the same thing spiritually and emotionally.

After His resurrection, Jesus appeared to His disciples in an upper room. They were terrified, locked in the room lest they suffer the same fate as their Lord. Suddenly, the risen Lord appeared in their midst. He showed them His hands and His side that had been pierced. He wanted them to look carefully at His wounds and ponder the miracle of redemption.

What is so significant about His wounds suffered on the cross? The wounds are the physical evidence of betrayal and rejection. While His closest friends had not directly rejected Him, they did abandon Him in Gethsemane when He was arrested. Peter went so far as to deny Him.

It was difficult for them to look at His wounds because of their guilt. Yet, as He showed them His wounded hands, feet and side, He said, "Peace be with you!" (John 20:19). He never mentioned their failure. He never asked them to admit their guilt. He had already released them, and His announcement was, Peace! Then He instructed them to carry His gospel to the world. It was His forgiveness that helped them get over their failure and repurpose their lives.

Are we quick to announce peace when we are wounded? Are we as liberal as Jesus with our forgiveness? Often we want people to pay us back, apologize and admit they were wrong. We want to punish them and see them get what they deserve. But there is a more excellent way: "Do not take revenge, my friends, but leave room for God's wrath, for it is written, 'It is mine to avenge; I will repay,' says the Lord" (Romans 12:19). Humans can't be trusted with vengeance. That is God's prerogative if He so chooses. Our role is to forgive.

> If we demand justice be served against those who hurt us, we can only expect justice for ourselves.

Jesus cautions, "Do not judge so that you will not be judged" (Matthew 7:1, *NASB*). The judgment we place upon others will return to us. Resentment leads us down the destructive path of a judgmental life.

Justice is a tricky thing. If we demand justice be served against those who hurt us, we can only expect justice for ourselves. Honestly, do we really want God to deal justly? Would not we rather have mercy? Let us be merciful toward others, as we desire for God to be merciful toward us. "Blessed are the merciful, for they will be shown mercy" (Matthew 5:7).

The most radical statement Jesus ever made about love is, "Love your enemies" (Luke 6:27). Anybody can love his friends. Anybody can love those who love him in return. But the proof of true discipleship is love without limits. Listen to the advice of James on this matter of mercy:

> If you really keep the royal law found in Scripture, "Love your neighbor as yourself," you are doing right. . . . Speak and act as those who are going to be judged by the law that gives freedom, because judgment without mercy will be shown to anyone who has not been merciful. Mercy triumphs over judgment! (James 2:8, 12, 13).

Two verses in the Psalms concerning the nature of God have always fascinated me. First, "His anger lasts only a moment" (Psalm 30:5). Second, "His mercy is everlasting" (Psalm 100:5, *NKJV*).

Love is the supreme command of Jesus. "A new commandment I give you: Love one another. As I have loved you so you must love one another" (John 13:34). Love like Jesus loves. Forgive like Jesus forgives. Be merciful as Jesus is merciful. We all get angry, and we all suffer hurt. But let us be like our Father in heaven, angry only for a moment. Quickly resolve feelings of anger and hurt lest they turn into resentment. Mercy always triumphs over judgment!

I sat in a ministers' meeting listening to a conversation about how the organization should discipline and restore ministers who suffer moral failure. I cringed as I listened to some ministers insist we should "toe the line on sin" and "make it hard" for those who fall. "Some sins are beyond restoration," one man thundered angrily.

I realized that is exactly how they see God. To them, everything is hard and difficult, with little or no margin for error. Contrasted to their stern words were those of men calling for mercy and a second chance. In my heart I pondered the words of God, "I desire mercy, not sacrifice" (Hosea 6:6) and the self-disclosure of Jesus, "My yoke is easy and my burden is light" (Matthew 11:30).

Repurposing your life means releasing the baggage of resentment and learning to travel light. Pause now, and

> **Repurposing your life means releasing the baggage of resentment and learning to travel light.**

bring those people who have hurt you before God in prayer: "Father, I forgive them for every hurtful thing they have said or done against me. Bless them abundantly. May they know you fully as their Lord. I entrust them to You. Amen."

Whenever any feelings of resentment resurface, tell yourself: "I have forgiven and released that person. He

(she) owes me nothing. I love and pray for him (her)."
Resentment will flee.

You can repurpose your life through the power of forgiveness. Cast off the unfinished business of the past and
move on to the new life God has for you.

Chapter 4

Facing Your Fears

Facing Your Fears

trike one. Sparky was a terrible student. After failing every subject in the eighth grade, he moved on to high school where he flunked Latin, algebra and English, and scored a zero in physics.

Strike two. Sparky wasn't any good at sports. The only team he made was the golf team, and he lost the only important game of the season.

Strike three. Sparky didn't have many friends. Nobody at school loved him or hated him; they simply didn't care that much. Fear of rejection kept him from approaching girls, and he didn't have a single date in high school.

With three strikes against him, Sparky thought he was a loser and so did everyone else, but this did not cause him to abandon all hope for future success. He knew if he were destined to be a success, he would be. If not, he would do the one thing that made him happy—draw cartoons.

He submitted some cartoons to the yearbook committee

at his high school, but they were rejected. In spite of this, Sparky loved drawing so much he decided to become a professional artist.

After graduation from high school, Sparky's first step was to send a letter to Walt Disney Studios regarding his ambitions. He was given a topic and asked to send some sample cartoons about that topic. He did so and was quickly rejected again.

Sparky still didn't give up. Instead, he decided to write an autobiography using cartoons. He drew the story of an unsuccessful little boy who always seemed to fail. People who saw Sparky's cartoon soon grew to love this boy because he was so true to life.

The "Peanuts" comic strip and its star, Charlie Brown, became famous worldwide, as did their creator, whose real name was Charles Schulz. Because of his perseverance and hope, "Sparky" was able to face his fears and emerge victorious.[1]

We all face intimidation. To *intimidate* means "to make timid, cause fear, discourage or refrain from acting by making threats." Intimidation robs us of self-confidence and discourages us from trying to pursue our goals. When we are intimidated, we can lose the battle before we even start fighting by telling ourselves from the outset we're going to lose.

> Intimidation robs us of self-confidence and discourages us from trying to pursue our goals.

Intimidation can come from without or within. We can

be intimidated by people through rejection, ridicule or threats. Circumstances can also be intimidating. The chances of success may be so small we feel threatened or believe we are inadequate to meet the challenge.

A Shepherd Who Became King

One of the most beloved persons who ever lived was King David. The only way a humble shepherd could become king was to be successful in spite of fear and many intimidating situations.

David could have been intimidated by the call of God. At God's command, the prophet Samuel came to Jesse's house to find a king for Israel. Samuel first interviewed Jesse's seven oldest sons but God told Samuel that David, the youngest son, was the man God had chosen for the job (1 Samuel 16:1-13).

David's older brothers envied him and tried to intimidate him. According to 1 Samuel 17, David's father sent him to the battlefield where his brothers were serving in the Israelite army. The Israelite and Philistine armies had faced off in the valley of Elah, and the strongest Philistine warrior, Goliath, was strutting around near the battlefield and taunting the Israelite soldiers. He issued a tough challenge: He would take on the best Israelite soldier in one-on-one combat. If the Israelite won, the Philistines would surrender. If Goliath won, the Israelites would surrender. Nobody took the challenge. Every Israelite soldier was intimidated by the overpowering size of Goliath.

When young David heard the taunts of Goliath, he was outraged. Such threats against Israel or against the Lord would not be tolerated. David marched right up to King Saul's tent and boldly announced that he was the man for the job. His brothers tried to keep him from going—they tried to intimidate him. They ridiculed him and said he was only trying to get attention. David, like us, certainly wanted his family to believe in him, but he wasn't about to let their intimidation dissuade him.

Goliath tried to intimidate David when they squared off. Goliath, standing more than eight feet tall, mocked David, threatening to feed him to the birds. Unfazed, David snapped back at Goliath's taunts with confidence: "You come against me with sword and spear and javelin, but I come against you in the name of the Lord Almighty" (v. 45). With that he struck Goliath between the eyes with a stone hurled from his sling. Goliath fell like a mighty oak to the ground. David went over to the fallen giant, drew Goliath's own sword and cut off his head. Fear struck the Philistine army, and they scattered.

David defeated Goliath because he refused to be intimidated by anyone, including his family. As far as he was concerned, he and God constituted a majority. Together, they could accomplish anything.

In 1 Samuel 18 and 19, King Saul envied David so much he tried to kill him, although David had served the king faithfully as his chief military statesman. But Saul was jealous of the favor David had with God and with the people. When David had to flee the palace for his life, he lived for months in the wilderness of Judea, forced to seek refuge with the Philistines (1 Samuel 27). In spite of his many hardships, David kept his confidence and faith in God's promise that one day he would be king.

David could have been intimidated by those who resisted his leadership. Although he was crowned as Judah's king, the 10 northern tribes of Israel rejected his leadership and refused to acknowledge him as king. Instead of lashing out at the northern tribes, he patiently waited for God to fulfill the promise. Finally, after seven years the whole nation was united under his leadership (2 Samuel 5:1-5).

David had plenty of reasons to be intimidated, but he faced his fears in faith, knowing God was sovereign. He knew God had called him to be king, even though he did not have the right family background, or the necessary training. God would make him adequate and competent for the task.

David gives us the secret to facing our fears in Psalm 27:1, "The Lord is my light and my salvation—whom shall I fear? The Lord is the stronghold of my life—of whom shall I be afraid?" Whenever you feel intimidated and your heart is filled with fear, confidently claim God's promise. You can know, beyond the shadow of any doubt, that God is with you, providing comfort and strength in difficult circumstances.

David understood this better than anyone. He goes on to say . . .

Though an army besiege me, my heart will not fear;
though war break out against me, even then will I be
confident. . . . For in the day of trouble he will keep me
safe in his dwelling; he will hide me in the shelter of his
tabernacle and set me high upon a rock. Then my head
will be exalted above the enemies who surround me
(Psalm 27:3, 5, 6).

What confidence in God! I reiterate: In David's mind,
he and God were a majority and no one could defeat
them, not even an entire army.

Although we should face life with confidence, we
should never let self-confidence replace our trust in God.

> Although we should face life with confidence, we should never let self-confidence replace our trust in God.

A man who had survived a
devastating flood talked
about it endlessly. When he
died and went to heaven,
St. Peter greeted him at the
pearly gates and said, "If
you think of anything that will make you happy here, just
mention it."

"Well, there is *one* thing," replied the man. "I'd like to
tell a group of people here about my experience in that
awful flood."

"I'm sure a number of people will be interested,"
replied Peter. "I will arrange a meeting." The following
evening a large group gathered to hear the man's story.
Just before the flood survivor went out to speak, St. Peter
tapped him on the shoulder and whispered, "I thought
you'd like to know that Noah is in the audience."

We need a healthy dose of God-inspired confidence to face the challenges of life.

Wait on the Lord

When David penned the words of Psalm 27, he was facing overwhelming odds. He mentions enemies, false witnesses and an army opposing him. He writes of being estranged from God's Temple in Jerusalem where he loved to go to pray and worship. He wrote this psalm while he was being chased like a criminal by Saul. The king he had loved and supported was now seeking his life. David had hit rock bottom.

How did he keep up his courage? The situation certainly warranted giving up hope, or questioning God, or lashing out at Saul in revenge. He chose, however, to trust God to work out everything for good. He concludes the psalm by sharing his secret to winning over intimidation: He learned to wait on the Lord.

What should you do when you have exhausted all resources and you're facing insurmountable odds? You should wait on the Lord—completely depend on His intervention in situations beyond your control.

Go back to David's opening words: "The Lord is my light." God is our source of life and guidance. Imagine you are lost in a dark cave. What would you most desperately need? Light. David had this in mind. He was trapped in the desert, often hiding in dark caves. In those times the Lord was his only light and source of direction. God was his way out.

The rhetorical question, "Whom shall I fear?" deserves our attention. It would do us well to make a list of our fears and measure them against the Lord who is our Light, our salvation and our refuge.

Be Strong

David gives himself a pep talk: "Be strong." This admonition is found throughout Scripture.

When the angel of the Lord appeared to Gideon, who was hiding in a threshing floor due to his fear, He addressed him as, "you mighty man of valor" (Judges 6:11, 12, *NKJV*). I'm sure Gideon looked around and responded, "Who—me?"

When God called Joshua to succeed Moses as the new leader of Israel and to lead them into the Promised Land (Joshua 1:1-9), I doubt he wanted the job. Would you want to follow Moses' act? It would be hard to top the parting of the Red Sea. No matter how great a leader Joshua was, he would always be second to Moses, and he knew it. But when God called Joshua to leadership, He instructed him three times, "Be strong and courageous" (Joshua 1:6, 7, 9, *NKJV*).

When God called Jeremiah to be a prophet, he responded to the Lord, "I am only a child" (Jeremiah 1:6). Yet God said, "I have made you a fortified city, an iron pillar and a bronze wall" (v. 18).

When Peter met Jesus, he told Him, "Depart from me, for I am a sinful man." Jesus replied, "Do not be afraid. From now on you will catch men" (Luke 5:8, 10, *NKJV*).

God also says to us: "Be strong! Be very courageous! The Lord your God is with you wherever you go." Remember Paul's encouragement: "If God is for us, who can be against us?" (Romans 8:31).

There are three parts to your self. First, there is the *outer self* that other people see. Then, there is the *inner self,* which is the way you see yourself. Finally, there is the *ideal self,* the person you dream of being. For every Christian, the ideal self is the self like Jesus. God wants your outer self, your inner self and your ideal self to be characterized by confidence.

> God wants your outer self, your inner self and your ideal self to be characterized by confidence.

Governor Christian Hertner was running hard for a second term in office. One day, after a busy day and no lunch, he arrived at a church barbecue. Hertner was famished. As the governor moved down the serving line, he held out his plate to the woman serving chicken. She put one piece on his plate and turned to the next person in line.

"Excuse me," Governor Hertner said, "do you mind if I have another piece of chicken?"

"Sorry, only one to a customer," said the woman.

The governor was a modest man, but he was also hungry, so he decided to throw a little weight around. "Lady, do you know who I am?" he said. "I'm the governor."

"And do you know who I am?" the woman responded. "I'm the lady in charge of the chicken. Now move along!"

Be strong! Give yourself a pep talk and a pat on the back from time to time. Even if you're the person serving the chicken, be strong and courageous! Here are some affirmations from Scripture to strengthen your courage.

- ◆ "March on, my soul; be strong!" (Judges 5:21).

- ◆ "Be strong and let us fight bravely for our people and the cities of our God. The Lord will do what is good in his sight" (2 Samuel 10:12).

- ◆ "Say to those with fearful hearts, 'Be strong, do not fear; your God will come, he will come with vengeance; with divine retribution he will come to save you'" (Isaiah 35:4).

- ◆ "Be strong in the Lord and the power of His might" (Ephesians 6:10, *NKJV*).

- ◆ "Be strong in the grace that is in Christ Jesus" (2 Timothy 2:1).

Sometimes people tag us with self-defeating labels. Take, for example, Adam Clarke, who was born in Ireland in the 18th century. His father once told a schoolteacher that Adam wouldn't do well in school. The teacher said, "He looks bright to me." That statement changed Adam's life. It let him out of the box his father had put him in. He lived to be 72 and became a great scholar, a Methodist preacher, and author of commentaries and the book *Clarke's Christian Theology.*

I read an inspiring story about Miami Dolphins head

coach Don Shula and his special teams coach Mike Westhoff. Westhoff tells of the time that Don Shula came to visit him in the hospital when Westhoff was suffering from bone cancer. Don came into his room while Mike was barely conscious after having surgery. "Thanks for coming, Coach."

"How are you doing?" Shula asked.

"Oh, OK." The mournful look in Westhoff's sunken eyes told a different story.

There was a long pause. Finally, Don leaned over closely and said, "Listen, Mike. I need you in training camp in July—on the field, ready to go. We're going all the way this year."

Later, Mike Westhoff recovered from bone cancer and continued as the special teams coach for the Dolphins. He would say of Shula, "I thought he would tuck me in, but he didn't. He treated me the way I could be, not the way I was."

You're stronger than you think, and you can handle more than you realize. God is not only with you and for you . . . God is *in you.* He is your source of strength.

Take Heart

Sometimes, you have to encourage yourself to keep from losing heart. To lose heart means to lose your faith, your resolve, your enthusiasm and your belief in God and in yourself.

When David volunteered to fight Goliath, he said to

King Saul, "Let no one lose heart on account of this Philistine; [I] will go and fight him" (1 Samuel 17:32).

The night Jesus came walking on the water to his disciples, he said, "Take courage! It is I. Don't be afraid" (Matthew 14:27). At the Last Supper he told his disciples, "Take heart! I have overcome the world" (John 16:33).

Confidence comes by spending time with God in prayer and in the Scripture. That's where David found his confidence. When he was being chased by Saul, he lived for a while in Ziklag, among the Philistines. He lost everything important to him. His own men turned against him. What did he do? At the moment of despair, "David found strength in the Lord his God" (1 Samuel 30:6). When no one else encouraged him, he found strength in God. That's how you take heart.

> Confidence comes by spending time with God in prayer and in the Scripture.

Fred Craddock tells of taking a short vacation in Gatlinburg, Tennessee, with his wife. One night they found a quiet little restaurant where they looked forward to a private meal. While they were waiting for their meal they noticed a distinguished-looking, white-haired man moving from table to table, visiting guests. Craddock whispered to his wife, "I hope he doesn't come over here." But the man did come by their table.

"Where you folks from?" he asked amicably.

"Oklahoma," they replied.

"Beautiful state, I hear, although I've never been there. What do you do for a living?"

Craddock said, "I teach homiletics at the graduate seminary of Phillips University."

"Oh, so you teach preachers, do you? Well, I've got a story I want to tell you." With that, he pulled up a chair and sat down at the table.

The man stuck out his hand. "I'm Ben Hooper. I was born not far away in these mountains. My mother wasn't married when I was born so I had a hard time growing up. When I started school my classmates had a name for me, and it wasn't very nice. I used to go off by myself during recess and lunchtime because their criticisms hurt so deeply. People in our little town wondered whose boy I was.

"When I was about 12 years old, a new preacher came to our church. I would always go in late and leave early, but one day the preacher said the benediction so fast I got caught and had to walk out with the crowd. I could feel every eye in the church on me. Just about the time I got to the door, I felt a big hand on my shoulder. I looked up, and the preacher was looking right at me.

"'Who are you, son? Whose boy are you?'

"I felt the old weight come down on me. It was like a big, black cloud. Even the preacher was putting me down.

"But as he looked down at me, studying my face, he smiled. 'Wait a minute,' he said, 'I know who you are. I see the family resemblance. You are a son of God.'

"With that he popped me across the rump and said, 'Boy, you've got a great inheritance. Go and claim it.'"

The old man looked across the table at Craddock and said, "That was the most important thing anyone ever said to me." With that, he shook their hands and moved on to another table to greet old friends.

Suddenly, Craddock remembered. On two occasions, the people of Tennessee had elected an illegitimate son to be their governor. His name was Ben Hooper.[2]

Chapter 5

Keeping Your Focus

Keeping Your Focus

other Teresa was once asked why people lose their spiritual passion. She replied simply, "Distractions."

An ancient adage says, "If you want to defeat them—distract them." Success in any endeavor requires focus. Without focus, we flounder.

Professional golfer Arnold Palmer recalls a lesson about overconfidence:

> It was the final hole of the 1961 Masters tournament, and I had a one-stroke lead and had just hit a very satisfying tee shot. As I approached my ball, I saw an old friend standing at the edge of the gallery. He motioned me over, stuck out his hand and said, "Congratulations." I took his hand and shook it, but as soon as I did, I knew I had lost my focus. On my next two shots, I hit the ball into a sand trap, then put it over the edge of the green. I missed a putt

and lost the Masters. You don't forget a mistake like that; you just learn from it and become determined that you will never do that again. I haven't in the 30 years since.[1]

Here is the formula for success:

A Clear Purpose + A Carefully Defined Plan of Action = Creative Power

All endeavors require an investment of energy. Energy is time, creativity and resources. There is a limited amount of energy available for any endeavor. Use your energy wisely. Define your purpose clearly and stick to the plan. Focus your energies on the "one thing" you want to achieve. Distractions, worries and doubts rob us of the energy we need to achieve our goals.

The task may be great or small. It may be to finish school, find a new job, take a mission trip, make a career change, answer the call to ministry, improve a marriage, or improve a relationship with one's children. Whatever your goal happens to be, focus on it with all your energy. "Whatever your hand finds to do, do it with all your might" (Ecclesiastes 9:10).

> Define your purpose clearly and stick to the plan. Focus your energies on the "one thing" you want to achieve.

The apostle Paul was a focused person. He kept his focus on God's purpose from the time he met Jesus on the Damascus Road until the day he was martyred in

Rome. His final words were: "I have fought the good fight, I have finished the race" (2 Timothy 4:7).

While the football fan was thrilled to be at the Super Bowl, he was disappointed with the location of his seat. Peering across the stadium, he spotted an empty seat on the 50-yard line and made his way there. He asked the man in the next seat over, "Do you mind if I sit here?"

"Go ahead," the man replied. "This was my wife's seat. She was a huge football fan, and we came to the games together all the time until she passed away."

"I'm sorry for your loss," the fan said. "But I'm curious. Why didn't you give the extra ticket to a friend or relative?"

The widower replied, "They're all at her funeral."

Now that's having the wrong focus!

Beware of Distractions

Beware of life's uncertainties. We need to stop being surprised by life's unexpected events. Whenever we pursue any goal, a host of unexpected things may arise and hinder our progress. We look too much for guarantees that everything will work out as planned instead of taking the risk of faith.

The apostle Peter tells believers, "Dear friends, do not be surprised at the painful trial you are suffering, as though something strange were happening to you. But rejoice that you participate in the sufferings of Christ" (1 Peter 4:12, 13).

Beware of life's hardships. Success is determined by the way we handle setbacks. Discouragement is the greatest enemy to fulfilling one's purpose. Hardships can make us bitter or better—we decide how we respond.

> **Success is determined by the way we handle setbacks.**

Trials can lead to discouragement and disillusionment. Be willing to pay the price of success. E. Stanley Jones said, "Bitterness comes to all. Sours some; sweetens others. I shall use it to sweeten my spirit."

Instead of running away from hardships, we are to endure them. "Endure hardship . . . like a good soldier of Jesus Christ" (2 Timothy 2:3). "Let us run with perseverance the race marked out for us" (Hebrews 12:1). "Blessed is the man who perseveres under trial, because when has stood the test, he will receive the crown of life that God has promised to those who love him" (James 1:12).

In his book, *Too Busy Not To Pray,* Bill Hybels shares a moving account of a man who kept his focus in the face of life's hardships:

> A couple of years ago, a member of my church's vocal team and I were invited by a Christian leader named Yesu to go to southern India. There we joined a team of people from various parts of the U.S. We were told that God would use us to reach Muslims and Hindus and nonreligious people for Christ. We all felt called by God to go, but none of us knew what to expect. When we arrived, Yesu met us and invited us to his home. Over the course of the next few days, he told us about his ministry.

Yesu's father, a dynamic leader and speaker, had started the mission in a Hindu-dominated area. One day a Hindu leader came to Yesu's father and asked for prayer. Eager to pray with him, hoping he would lead him to Christ, he took him into a private room, knelt down with him, closed his eyes and began to pray. While he was praying, the Hindu man reached into his robe, pulled out a knife and stabbed him repeatedly.

Yesu, hearing his father's screams, ran to help him. He held him in his arms as blood poured out onto the floor of the hut. Three days later, his father died. On his deathbed he said to his son, "Please tell that man that he is forgiven. Care for your mother and carry on this ministry. Do whatever it takes to win people to Christ.[2]

Focused to the Finish

Living with purpose means realizing God has given each of us a task to do. He has also provided us with talents and abilities. God has "given us everything we need for life and godliness" (2 Peter 1:3).

Frustration sets in when we get sidetracked from doing God's will. Joy comes when we live within the boundaries of our gifts and callings (Romans 11:29).

> Joy comes when we live within the boundaries of our gifts and callings.

Refuse to quit until you finish the task. Missionary David Livingstone said, "I determined to never stop until I had come to the end and achieved my purpose."

Let me ask you . . .

◆ What tasks has the Lord given you to do?

◆ Are you focused on the right tasks?

◆ Do you have a clearly defined path to complete the tasks?

◆ Have you determined to finish the work you began?

Jesus encouraged everyone to believe God for great and mighty things. "If you have faith as small as a mustard seed, you can say to this mountain, 'Move from here to there' and it will move. Nothing will be impossible for you" (Matthew 17:20).

Turning Problems Into Opportunities

The Chinese symbol for a crisis means danger, but it also means opportunity. Life is a matter of perception because problems are often opportunities in disguise.

The way we view our circumstances determines how we will respond. We handle situations differently when we approach them as opportunities instead of problems.

> Life is a matter of perception because problems are often opportunities in disguise.

Here's a story to illustrate my point. Two shoe salesmen went to South America to explore new business opportunities. When they arrived at a small town, they both sent messages back to the corporate office.

The first salesman, a negativist, said: "There's no

opportunity here. Most of the people don't wear shoes."
The second sent word: "Send as many shoes as possible. Everyone here needs a pair."

The problem with "problems" is that we are on the negative side of the ledger from the outset. Problems can seem overwhelming. However, opportunities challenge us to find creative solutions and take positive action. *Stop solving problems and start setting goals!*

Take losing weight for example. We start with a problem (being overweight). Next we look for a solution (one of a thousand diet programs). Now there's a joyful word—*diet*. Instead of "losing" something, why not focus on "gaining" something? Set your sights on getting in shape, feeling better, living healthy and increasing energy.

Or, consider getting out of debt—a popular concept lately. Debt used to be promoted as a way of "establishing credit." No one enjoys the process of getting out of debt. So, instead of setting a negative goal of getting out of debt, turn it into a positive goal, such as saving money, learning to invest, securing your financial future or establishing a budget.

Take the problem of poor communication and anger resolution as another example. Reframe the problem as an opportunity to learn more effective communication skills. Strive for the goal of being at peace at all times, and you will automatically get a grip on anger.

My wife, Barbie, and I were invited to speak at a minister's conference that addressed the subject, "How to

Resolve Conflict in the Church." We chose instead to title our presentation, "How to Maintain Peace in Your Relationships." Rather than focusing on the problem of conflict, we focused on the goal of peace.

> Strive for the goal of being at peace at all times, and you will automatically get a grip on anger.

Problems disappear when goals are reached. Problems are not the problem; they are symptoms of the real problem—the lack of goals. Problems come and go. Goals are permanent.

Goals are like stars; they are always there. Adversity is like the clouds; it can make our goals harder to see, but it is temporary and will move on. So keep your eyes on the stars. This is how we chart the course of our lives. "Run in such way as to get the prize" (1 Corinthians 9:24).

A Plan of Action

Here are seven steps to reaching goals.

Step 1—Personalize. Theodore Roosevelt said: "If you are not actively pursuing the person you want to be, then you are pursuing the person you don't want to be." What good is it to gain wealth or fame at the expense of your happiness, health or family? What good is it to achieve success at the expense of compromising your convictions?

Who you are is more important than what you do. Bill Gates of Microsoft has become a billionaire, but he has also become the largest charitable giver in the world. His success has made him a better person.

True success is the character we develop in the

process of reaching our goals. Billy Graham reached a pinnacle of influence in the 1950s due to massive media exposure. He was offered a $1 million deal by a major TV network to host a secular show. He turned the offer down to start his own Christian program.

He wanted to name it *The Billy Graham Show*, but his wife, Ruth, told him she didn't believe that was proper. She came up with the name, *The Hour of Decision,* which can still be heard on radio and seen on TV around the world. He became better, not just bigger.

Step 2—Prioritize. Time management is crucial to reaching goals. Jesus said, "Seek first the kingdom of God" (Matthew 6:33, *NKJV*). Before He sent the church on its mission, He told the believers to wait in Jerusalem to receive the Spirit. First things first.

"Don't get the cart before the horse," my

> True success is the character we develop in the process of reaching our goals.

mother was fond of saying. Distinguish between the immediately urgent and the eternally important, and stick to the latter.

Make a list of the five most important people in your life, the five most important goals, and the five most important tasks facing you. Invest your time in these people, goals and projects. Remember the 20/80 rule: *20 percent of efforts will produce 80 percent of results.* Don't work harder, work smarter through wise planning.

Step 3—Pray. In fact, "pray continually" (1 Thessalonians 5:17). Submit your goals to the great purpose of

God with the prayer of Jesus: "Not My will, but Yours, be done" (Luke 22:42, *NKJV*). Begin every day with prayer and Scripture reading. "Let the word of Christ dwell in you richly as you teach and admonish one another with all wisdom" (Colossians 3:16).

Prayer enables you to adjust your attitude for the day or face the challenge at hand. Pray the Lord's Prayer every day and make it your ambition in life to fulfill it: "Your kingdom come. Your will be done" (Matthew 6:10, *NKJV*). When we pray, God puts dreams in our hearts. Prayer is God's pathway to creative planning and peaceful living. God guides the human heart in the secret place of prayer.

Sit quietly in the presence of God and listen for His still small voice. "In quietness and trust is your strength" (Isaiah 30:15). We hear God only in solitude and quietness. "Whether you turn to the right or to the left, your ears will hear a voice behind you, saying, 'This is the way; walk in it'" (Isaiah 30:21).

> Prayer enables you to adjust your attitude for the day or face the challenge at hand.

During Super Bowl XXVII in 1993, a Dallas Cowboys lineman named Leon Lett recovered a fumble and began dancing on his way to the end zone. But the ball was stripped from his hand at the goal line, and he failed to score the touchdown. The moral of the story is, "Don't let up!" Jesus taught the disciples, "Always pray and never give up" (Luke 18:1). Prayer is our lifeline to God. Without it, we are left powerless to meet life's demands and pressures, but when we pray we become larger than life.

Step 4—Plan. Use these five rules when setting goals:

1. *Goals need to be specific.* The best way to specify goals is to write them down. Only then are they clear enough for us to be fully committed to them.

2. *Goals need to be realistic.* There's no point trying to be the next Luciano Pavarotti if you can't carry a tune in a bucket. Go for goals that are within your reach.

3. *Goals are both short-range and long-range.* Make a list of both short-range goals (within a five-year period) and long-range goals (for some time farther in the future). Life moves in seasons. Dream now about what you would like to do in the next season of your life. Don't let the changes of life catch you by surprise.

4. *Goals need to be flexible.* Goals need to be reevaluated and revised periodically. Life-situations change and warrant the readjustment of goals. Life itself, like a financial portfolio, needs to be reviewed and possibly modified at least once a year.

5. *Goals need to be measurable.* Monitor your progress. Keep a written record so you can see how far you've come toward reaching your goals.

Step 5—Prize. Whenever you reach a goal, reward yourself for a job well done. Do something you enjoy. Always celebrate success. We spend too much time punishing ourselves for our mistakes and not enough time rewarding our successes. Sometimes you just have to encourage yourself.

Step 6—Participate. Share your goals with the important people in your life. Ask them to pray for you, hold you accountable and give you feedback on your progress. The Bible says, "Two are better than one, because they have a good return for their work: If one falls down, his friend can help him up. But pity the man who falls and has no one to help him up!" (Ecclesiastes 4:9, 10).

> We spend too much time punishing ourselves for mistakes and not enough time rewarding our successes.

Now, there may be times when you have to pursue your goals alone. People may not share your vision. I heard T.D. Jakes preach a masterful sermon recently entitled, "You Don't Have to Believe in My Dream." The point was, while people are helpful, they are not necessary to doing what God has called us to do. It is good to have support when you can get it, but God is the source of victory.

Step 7—Persevere. While many ingredients go into baking the success cake, none are more vital than hard work and perseverance. Someone gave me a letter opener for Christmas engraved with the words, "Never give up," three times. "Let us run with perseverance the race marked out for us" (Hebrews 12:1).

World-famous tenor Luciano Pavarotti relates this story.

When I was a boy, my father, a baker, introduced me to the wonders of song. He urged me to work very hard to develop my voice. Arrigo Pola, a professional tenor in my hometown of Modena, Italy, took me as a pupil. I also enrolled in a teachers' college. On graduating, I asked my father, "Shall I be a teacher or a singer?"

"Luciano," my father replied, "if you try to sit on two chairs, you will fall between them. For life, you must choose one chair."

I chose one. It took seven years of study and frustration before I made my first professional appearance. It took another seven to reach the Metropolitan Opera. And now I think whether it's laying bricks, writing a book— whatever we choose—we should give ourselves to it. Commitment, that's the key. Choose one chair.

Repurposing your life takes focus. So remember the formula:

A Clear Purpose +
A Carefully Defined Plan of Action =
Creative Power

Chapter 6

Finding Your Place

Finding Your Place

*I*n February 1980, the U.S. Olympic hockey team slipped its foot into a glass slipper and walked away with a gold medal at Lake Placid, New York. Those college athletes shocked the world by upsetting the powerful Soviet team, and then seized the championship from Finland while the crowd chanted, "USA!"

Before his team's victory over the Soviet Union, which advanced them to the finals, Herb Brooks, the coach of the U.S. hockey team, told each of his players, "You are born to be a player. You are meant to be here at this time. This is your moment."

You too can live with such a sense of destiny. We sometimes refer to it as a feeling of significance.

Our deepest emotional need is to be loved. Only when we are loved do we experience emotional and spiritual health and become free to love in return. Love gives us the sense of security and significance we desperately seek.

The need for love is met primarily through our parents. The first crisis newborn infants face is learning to either trust or mistrust the world around them. If the home is stable and nurturing, children see the world as a safe place and they feel secure. If, however, the climate is overbearing, harsh and lacking affection, children learn to be afraid. As adults, they battle anxiety and mistrust of people and institutions, always on the lookout for hidden agendas and ulterior motives.

> Only when we are loved do we experience emotional and spiritual health and become free to love in return.

Love brings feelings of significance and security. Parents who encourage their children impart to them courage and confidence. Love makes us believe we have something to contribute to the world. Parents who berate, criticize or ridicule a child, however, break the child's spirit and produce deeply rooted feelings of insignificance.

Peers are our second source of love. Entering school as a young child can be either terrific or terrifying. We all have mixed feelings about those early school days. Some memories we cherish and others we wish we could forget.

Feelings of security and significance are either enhanced or stifled in the critical years of childhood and adolescence. The adult years—characterized by marriage, raising children and building a career—bring experiences that can strengthen or destroy our sense of significance.

We must remember God himself is the ultimate source of love. "Perfect love drives out fear" (1 John 4:18).

Life-changing Insights

This prayer of the apostle Paul will help you know the magnitude of the love of God so you can discover a life of significance:

> I pray that you, being rooted and established in love, may have power, together with all the saints, to grasp how wide and long and high and deep is the love of Christ, and to know this love that surpasses knowledge—that you may be filled to the measure of all the fullness of God (Ephesians 3:17-19).

We envision Paul on his knees praying fervently that the Holy Spirit reveal to us the love of God. Why is Paul so impassioned about God's love? He knew that, without knowledge of God's love, we can never grow spiritually.

We need to be "rooted and established in love" (v. 17). When we are rooted in God's love, adversity and disappointment are handled with wisdom and patience.

> When we are rooted in God's love, adversity and disappointment are handled with wisdom and patience.

Apart from the knowledge of love, people blame God when adversity comes. "How can God love me and let this happen?" we ask.

Job said, "Though He slay me, yet will I trust Him" (Job 13:15, *NKJV*). He was rooted in love. Although he didn't understand his sufferings, he did understand that God loved and cared about him. When life is uncertain, one fact remains: *God is love* (1 John 4:16).

We need to move from an *awareness* of God's love to a full *assurance* of His love. When Paul prayed for us to know God's love, he wanted us to know by way of personal experience and on an emotional level. Not only are we to know His love, but also we are to tightly grasp His love and never let it go.

Yet, the love of God is a love that is beyond fully knowing. What a

Love makes us mature and complete—spiritually, emotionally and relationally.

paradox. Paul prays that we will know the love that surpasses knowledge. As long as we live, we will ponder the height, depth, length and width of God's love, because God loves us more deeply and more profoundly than we can ever begin to understand.

Such knowledge fills us with all the fullness of God. Love makes us mature and complete—spiritually, emotionally and relationally. The Beatles were right after all, "All you need is love." But it is the love of God that counts.

Covenant Love

My breakthrough in understanding God's love came with the birth of my son, David Paul. Standing in the delivery room, holding our firstborn in my arms, my heart was flooded with a love too great for words. As I looked into the face of our baby boy and saw my own likeness in his features, the Scripture danced in my mind: "God created man in his own image" (Genesis 1:27).

Suddenly, I realized if I could feel such love for my son, God loved me as much as His Son. I have never doubted God's love since. His love frees us from all fears, empowering us to face confidently every challenge life brings us.

God's love is a covenant love. A *covenant* is an unconditional vow on the part of someone who is benevolent toward another. The Hebrew word for *love* is *hesed* and means a strong, steadfast and loyal love. Covenant love is unfailing love.

A man said to his friend at work, "You and your wife are having a wedding anniversary soon, right?"

"Yeah, that's right," the man said. "It's a big one—20 years."

His friend replied, "What are you going to do for your wife on your anniversary?"

"I'm taking her on an exotic trip to Australia."

"Wow, Australia, that's some gift," his friend replied. "That's going to be hard to beat. What are you going to do for your 25th anniversary?"

The man said, "Go back and get her."

That's far from God's unconditional love, which is not based on our performance. From the time we are small children, we learn to perform for love. Parents are forever trying to make their children perform. "What do you say?" "Say thank you." "Tell him your name." "Tell them how old you are." Of course, children rarely perform on cue. They intentionally make their parents look bad by refusing to perform. Sadly, we apply this principle all through life, performing for approval, affirmation and love.

Here are two truths you need to know: You cannot do anything good enough to make God love you more. You cannot do anything bad enough to make God love you less. Of course, I'm not advocating irresponsibility. Our actions certainly have consequences. My point is, however, that the only true constant in life is the love of God. God not only loves us, He *is* love!

I'm reminded of a Dennis the Menace comic strip. Dennis and his friend Joey are pictured leaving Mrs. Wilson's house with their hands full of cookies. Joey says to Dennis, "I wonder what we did to deserve this?"

Dennis responds, "Look, Joey, Mrs. Wilson gives us cookies not because we're nice, but because she's nice." So it is with God. He loves us because of who He is, not because of who we are or what we do.

Everlasting Love

Our concept of eternity is that it begins in the present and continues forever. But eternity is not only without end, it is also without beginning. Eternity is circular as is God's love.

More than twenty years ago I met my wife, Barbie, on a blind date. I fell in love with her the moment I laid eyes on her. Her beauty was captivating. It was love at first sight—at least it was for me. She says it took a little longer for her.

I lost all sense of rhyme and reason. I was *madly* in love. There's nothing more euphoric than falling in love. Eleven days after that blind date I asked her to marry me. There's nothing like knowing what you want! Of course, she said yes.

I will love her for eternity. But my love for Barbie had a beginning—a blind date. It was the only one I ever had. By the way—see how risky a blind date can be!

I saw Barbie and immediately fell in love with her, but God's love is not like that. He did not decide one day He loved us. His love is eternal, with no beginning. God loved us before we were born.

Just as His love has no beginning, it also has no end. His love is not based on our behavior, success, personality or morality. His love is not the result of who we are but who He is.

Notice Paul's insights: "For he chose us in him before the creation of the world to be holy and blameless in his sight. In love, he predestined us to adopted as his sons" (Ephesians 1:4). Think of it—God chose us as His own before the dawn of creation.

God told the young prophet Jeremiah: "Before I formed you in the womb I knew you, before you were born I set you apart; I appointed you as a prophet to the nations" (Jeremiah 1:5). As Jeremiah came to understand the eternal love of God, he was able share it with others. When the nation of Judah had broken their covenant with

God, His love drew them back: "I have loved you with an everlasting love; I have drawn you with loving-kindness" (31:3). There's the Hebrew word *hesed* again—"loving-kindness."

Covenant love is the love that will not let you go. It keeps pursuing us when we wander away from God.

> Covenant love keeps pursuing us when we wander away from God.

His love draws us and seeks us out. God didn't notice your beauty, talent or net worth one day and decide to love you. He has and always will love you. His love is an everlasting love.

Sacrificial Love

Can we truly understand the love of God without considering His sacrifice? The essential nature of love is sacrifice. If we had to summarize the Bible's message in one verse, we would be left with the words of Jesus: "God so loved the world that he gave his one and only Son" (John 3:16).

Paul's confession of faith celebrates Jesus' sacrificial love. "I live by faith in the Son of God, who loved me and gave himself for me" (Galatians 2:20).

The apostle John was known as the apostle of love. He knew that love is an elusive concept, but he provided the essential definition of true love: "This is love: not that we loved God, but that he loved us and sent his Son as an atoning sacrifice for our sins" (1 John 4:10).

Feelings of insecurity and insignificance melt away

with one look at the Cross. While joy comes from looking upward and outward, depression comes from looking
inward. It sets in when the mind is engrossed in mulling
over one's sins, failures and disappointments.

Look at the Cross. The Son of God paid the penalty
for your sins. You are worth the sacrifice of the Son of
God. Calvary is the ultimate measure of a person's
worth.

A Scottish theologian named John Duncan of New
College in Edinburgh once attended a service held in a
church in Scotland. As Holy Communion was being
served, he noticed that a young girl turned her head away
as the elements came to her. She motioned for the elder
serving to take the cup away—that she couldn't drink it.
When he realized what was happening, Duncan reached
out his hand, touched her shoulder and said, "Take it,
sweetheart. It's for sinners."

Unconditional Love

A wide chasm exists between human and divine love.
Human love is *love because of.* "I love you because
you're beautiful or rich or because of what you can do for
me." Human love is *love if.* "I love you if you're pretty, if
you meet my needs, or if you change and become the person I want you to be." Human love tends to manipulate,
exploit and control in order to get what it wants.

Divine love is *love in spite of.* God loves in spite of our
sins and failures. God doesn't love because He wants

something from us, but because we are His children. "God demonstrates his own love for us in this: While we were still sinners, Christ died for us" (Romans 5:8).

Profound words worth pondering—"while we were still sinners." While we were unlovable, Christ died for us. While we were undeserving, Christ died for us. While we were transgressing God's law, Christ died for us.

Because we tend not to love ourselves, we project our feelings of self-loathing onto God, assuming wrongly He doesn't love us either. Our distortions of God's love often result from negative feelings about ourselves or from the negative ways we have been treated. If we are basically afraid of God and don't really believe He loves us, we try to make ourselves lovable to Him the way a child does— earning approval.

> God doesn't love because He wants something from us, but because we are His children.

God loves unconditionally. No strings attached. We have a tough time believing that because human love is conditional. We love with strings attached. We try not to, but we do. We look for the return on our investment. We expect love in return, but not God. He loves because He is love. God even likes us! He created us that we might enjoy His presence and that He might enjoy ours.

Abby sat in my office dejected. I listened compassionately as she shared with me the deep scars left by her divorce some 10 years earlier. Her husband had been unfaithful and, when she finally got the truth out of him, she was devastated. As bad as the hurt was, she still loved him and she wanted their marriage healed. But he wanted nothing of the same. He promptly told her he had no intention of reconciling their marriage and, over the next few months, pushed the divorce through as quickly as possible.

Having been raised in a strict religious home that frowned on divorce under any and every circumstance, she abandoned any hope for a second chance. In her mind, to remarry would be to live in adultery and out of the will of God. She would have to wear the scarlet letter "*D*," living as a marked woman for the rest of her life.

The problem was, she wanted to remarry. She was young, had her whole life ahead of her and longed for a Christian husband with whom she could share her life. But how could she ever get past the guilt and shame of being divorced? Would God ever permit her to remarry and grant her His blessing? These were the questions that filled her mind that day as we talked.

She then asked me one of the most heartbreaking questions I've ever been asked. "Can God ever use me for His glory since I've been divorced?"

As I listened intently to Abby's dilemma, sensing her despair, I was so glad I could give her hope—a way out of her pain. She could have hope because God is the God of a second chance. And a third chance, and a fourth chance, and on and on.

She couldn't control her husband's decision to have an affair and divorce her in order to be with another woman.

That wasn't her fault. Furthermore, she was free to remarry. Most importantly, I reassured her that God would still use her for His glory—she was not disqualified from the prize. She found freedom from guilt and shame in the light of God's love.

Secure Love

God will keep us securely in his love. He "is able to keep you from falling and to present you before his glorious presence without fault and with great joy" (Jude 24). While I meet people who struggle with eternal security, I meet even more who battle the feeling of eternal insecurity. God's love is the only antidote to insecurity.

> While I meet people who struggle with eternal security, I meet even more who battle the feeling of eternal insecurity. God's love is the only antidote to insecurity.

Theologian Karl Barth served as both pastor and professor in Germany during the mid-20th century. His theological works continue to inspire readers. He made a single visit to the U.S. in the early 60s and preached in Miller Chapel at Princeton University.

Following the service, a visiting newspaper reporter stopped him on the steps outside and asked him, "Could you sum up your theology in one statement?"

By this time, Barth had completed the first 10 volumes of *Church Dogmatics*—over 8,000 pages of nearly impenetrable doctrinal exposition. Now he was being asked to boil it all down to one sentence.

He looked squarely at the reporter and answered, "Jesus loves me, this I know, for the Bible tells me so."

Purposeful living doesn't come from what you do, but from who you are as a person made in the image of God and knowing you are loved by God. "How great is the love the Father has lavished on us, that we should be called children of God! And that is what we are!" (1 John 3:1).

Chapter 7

Bouncing Back
From Your Setbacks

*W*inston Churchill once said, "Success is going from one failure to the next without a loss of enthusiasm." Success is largely determined by the way we handle failure.

When Thomas Edison invented the light bulb, he tried over 2,000 experiments before he was successful. A young reporter asked him how he felt after failing so many times. He said, "I never failed once. I invented the light bulb. It just happened to be a 2,000-step process."

Some people feel as though success will never be theirs. They're like the guy who said, "I've come to the conclusion that the key to success just doesn't fit my ignition." They consider themselves inadequate for the challenge, lacking the necessary resources or facing too many obstacles to reach their goals. Consequently, they stop dreaming, drift with the tide and accept the status quo.

Failure constitutes an integral part of success. John D.

Rockefeller, Sr. got into a city cab one day on his way to a meeting. The cabbie recognized him and asked, "Sir, I have some money to invest. Can you advise me?"

"Sure," replied Rockefeller. "You need to make good decisions."

The cabbie responded, "Thanks for the tip, but how can I learn to make good decisions?"

"Experience," came Rockefeller's reply.

"How can I get experience?" asked the cabbie.

Rockefeller replied, "By making bad decisions."

I was once asked to write a chapter in a book on "Failures in the Ministry." They should have asked me to write the whole book! Like you, I know the pain of failure in both life and ministry. Unfulfilled dreams. Sermons gone awry. Plans that bombed. Personnel decisions that backfired. Unsupportive leaders. Financial setbacks. Building program hassles. Time management struggles. Conquering enemies without, only to lose the war within.

> **Failure provides a unique opportunity for the glory of God to be demonstrated in our lives.**

Above all, we need to understand that failure provides a unique opportunity for God's glory to be demonstrated. As John F. Kennedy observed in his book, *Profiles in Courage,* "Great crises produce great men and great deeds of courage." Failure is often the chisel God uses to sculpt us into great men and women for His glory.

The apostle Paul understood this vital truth. He reminds everyone in ministry,

If you only look at us, you might well miss the brightness. We carry this precious Message around in the unadorned clay pots of our ordinary lives. That's to prevent anyone from confusing God's incomparable power in us. As it is, there's not much chance of that. You know for yourselves that we're not much to look at. We've been surrounded and battered by troubles, but we're not demoralized; we're not sure what to do, but we know that God knows what to do; we've been spiritually terrorized, but God hasn't left our side; we've been thrown down, but we haven't broken (2 Corinthians 4:7-9, *TM*).

From Fisherman to Failure

The apostle Peter is one of the most colorful personalities in the New Testament. His life and ministry were marked by great moments and flashes of success.

He was personally called by Jesus. He let down his net for the miracle catch of fish. He possessed keen insight into Christ's divinity as evidenced by his confession, "You are the Christ, the Son of the living God" (Matthew 16:16). He walked with Jesus on the water. He showed his loyalty to Jesus in Gethsemane by taking up his sword and cutting off a soldier's ear. He was probably aiming for his head! He preached confidently on the Day of Pentecost, resulting in 3,000 conversions. His shadow healed those in the streets of Jerusalem. He raised a woman from the dead in Joppa, resulting in a citywide revival.

Not a bad résumé.

Yet, these peak experiences were tempered by valleys of defeat. He denied his Lord. He lacked courage to embrace the Cross. His fear of rejection along with his need to be accepted won the battle against his devotion to Jesus. He could follow Christ to feed the multitudes, heal the sick, raise the dead and calm the storm. But he couldn't follow Him to the cross.

As Jesus was led to Pilate's Hall of Judgment, Luke simply records, "Peter followed at a distance" (22:54). That says it all, doesn't it? His spirit was willing but his flesh was weak. When Christ needed him most, Peter was nowhere to be found.

His denial ushered in a tidal wave of guilt and discouragement. After Jesus died, he told the disciples, "I'm going out to fish" (John 21:3). In essence, he was saying: "Enough of this ministry business. I don't have what it takes. I'm going back to my comfort zone, the fishing trade, where I don't have to risk failure again. The demands are too great; the requirements too exacting."

Failure is no stranger to us. We've all said yes when we vowed we would say no. We've yielded when we resolved to stand our ground. We've surrendered when we were determined to fight. We too have felt the shame. The guilt. The inadequacy.. We too have said, "I'm going out to fish."

From Failure to Faithful

But Peter bounced back! One of the most moving

narratives of Jesus in John's Gospel is his restoring Peter to the ministry (see John 21:1-23). Having fished all night, the first voice the discouraged disciples heard in the early morning hour was the majestic voice of Jesus penetrating the cool morning mist. "Friends, haven't you any fish?" (v. 5).

Have you ever noticed that, every time the Bible records the disciples fishing, they caught nothing? Apparently, they were just as bad at fishing as they were at preaching! Perhaps that explains why, when Jesus first called them to follow Him, "They *immediately* left their nets and followed Him" (Matthew 4:20, emphasis added). I guess they were eager to try their hands at a new profession.

A few early morning hours on the Galilean shore with Jesus revolutionized Peter's life. He learned how to handle failure and so can we.

Timeless Truths

1. *Failure is never final.* "Early in the morning," Jesus came to them (John 21:4). The morning speaks of a new day. A new opportunity. A new start. "His mercies begin afresh each day" (Lamentations 3:24, *NLT*). Paul reminds us, "Therefore, if anyone is in Christ, he is a new creation; the old has gone, the new has come!" (2 Corinthians 5:17).

God is the God of a second chance. And a third chance. And on and on.

What a fantastic affirmation to face every morning: "The old has gone, the new has come!"

Remember Jonah? He is not exactly a prime example of single-minded obedience. He ran from God and refused his ministry assignment. But God outran him. Jonah repented of his prejudice against the people of Nineveh and submitted to God's will. After that, the Book of Jonah records this simple yet profoundly reassuring truth: "Then the word of the Lord came to Jonah *a second time*" (3:1, emphasis added). What a promise! God speaks *a second time* when we fail.

A farmer had an apple tree that had been uprooted by the wind. A passer-by asked him, "What are you going to do with the tree?"

The farmer replied, "I am going to gather the fruit and then burn the tree." So it is with failure. Gather the fruit—learn what you can. Then, burn the tree—put the past behind you.

2. *Failure does not change our status with the Lord.* "Friends," Jesus called to the disciples from the water's edge. What a beautiful word—friends. The night of the Last Supper, Jesus said, "I no longer call you servants. . . . Instead, I have called you friends" (John 15:15). By calling the disciples "friends" that morning by the sea, Jesus reassured them that their relationship was still intact.

When we fail, we tend to convince ourselves that God can never use us again—that He puts us on the shelf and affixes to us the label, "vessel of dishonor." If you haven't not-iced, the Pharisees are still alive and well in our midst. They want to brand fallen leaders with the scarlet letter, "*F*" for failure.

God uses us in spite of our imperfections. If God didn't use imperfect people, nothing would be accomplished. After all, those are the only people available. You are not a second-class citizen or a vessel of dishonor because you have failed. His calling is still on your life as it was on Peter's. "God's gifts and his call are irrevocable" (Romans 11:29). Granted, you may need a season of healing and restoration to prepare you for effective service again, but God's call remains.

> God uses us in spite of our imperfections. If God didn't use imperfect people, nothing would be accomplished.

Jesus teaches us about God's incredible love in His parable of the Prodigal Son. You know the story. The younger son squandered his inheritance living in the fast lane. When the money ran out, so did his friends. Alone, broke and ashamed of what he'd become, he decided to return home. But how could he ever face his father again? What would he say to him? "I will arise and go to my father, and I will say to him, 'Father, I have sinned against heaven and before you, and I am no longer worthy to be called your son. Make me like one of your hired servants'" (Luke 15:18, 19, *NKJV*). In his mind, his failure changed his status from a son to a servant.

When he arrived home, however, his father would hear none of it. Running out of the house to greet his boy as soon as he saw him coming down the road, he called to the servants, "My son was dead and is alive again; he was lost and is found" (v. 24, *NKJV*). The young man said, "Make me a servant." The father said, "My son."

3. *Failure can be transformed into success.* Jesus called to the disciples, "Have you caught anything?" "Nothing," came the reply. They felt like one big zero. Nothing.

When Jesus asks you, "Have you caught anything?" you may hang your head and say, "Nothing." There's the problem. We make the mistake of measuring our worth by our accomplishments only to assess the results and say, "We've caught nothing."

Yet, in the midst of real or imagined failure, Jesus says, "Throw the net in on the right side." The disciples obeyed him, and this time they caught more fish than they could handle. The miracle had a message: "Get up and try again." Jesus speaks to us in our failures and says, "Throw your net in again." Don't quit. He still gives miracle-grace to transform failure into success.

Jesus taught to pray always and *never give up.* Paul assures us, "We will reap a harvest if we *do not give up*" (Galatians 6:9, emphasis added).

On October 29, 1941, Winston Churchill delivered a speech at his alma mater, Harrow School. His speech included these immortalized words: "Never give in. Never give in. Never, never, never, never—in nothing, great or small, large or petty—never give in, except to convictions of honor and good sense."

When James J. Corbett won the heavyweight boxing championship in 1892, he was asked, "What was your strategy to win the championship?"

Corbett responded, "When I was hit so hard that my head was ringing and my eyes were swollen shut, I would tell myself, 'Box one more round.' When I found myself lying on the mat hearing the 10-count, I would tell myself, 'Box one more round.' Somehow I have always found the strength and determination to box another round. I became the heavyweight champion of the world because I always box one more round."

Box one more round! This was what Jesus was telling those fishermen that day. In spite of the fact that you've caught nothing—throw in your net again.

4. *To fail is not to be a failure.* By the time the disciples arrived on shore with the fish, Jesus already had breakfast prepared. "Come and have breakfast," he said (v. 12). Why did he bother to fix them breakfast? The meal represents a restored relationship. Jesus fed the multitude with bread and fish. He broke the bread at the Passover. He shared a meal with two of the disciples after his resurrection on the Emmaus Road. He offered the same covenant meal to the Laodiceans who had failed: "I will go in and eat with him, and he with me" (Revelation 3:20).

> Present failure does not negate past success nor does it prevent future greatness. So, take the risk again.

The point is, one failure or a series of failures does not make your entire life a failure. Present failure does not negate past success nor does it prevent future greatness. So, take the risk again.

5. *Failure does not disqualify us from service in the kingdom.* In fact, sometimes failure leads to the broken-ness required to make us fit for service. There is no gold without the refiner's fire, no diamond without the stone-cutter's tool, no vessel without the potter's pliable clay.

I suppose if Peter kept a journal of his experiences with failure it would read something like this:

I never dreamed it could have happened to me. How could I have misjudged my own character to this extent?

I was one of the first people that He called to follow Him. It wasn't long until people in the group looked to me as a leader. I was outspoken, courageous and even popular. On one occasion, the Master himself said I would possess the very keys of the kingdom of heaven.

But I failed Him. I let Him down when He needed me most.

I really thought I was committed to Him, but what a rude awakening that awful night in Gethsemane was for me.

Supper had been so enjoyable. Celebrating the Passover with the Master was always special. In fact, the entire week was one of the most memorable occasions in all my life.

As He rode into Jerusalem, the people waved palm branches and shouted in praise: "Hosanna! Blessed is

He who comes in the name of the Lord."

He did such extraordinary things that week, like cursing the fig tree on the way to Lazarus' home in Bethany and driving the moneychangers from the temple courts. I had never seen that side of Him before.

His teaching was of a different nature that week as well. The religious leaders confronted Him on several occasions, plotting to trap Him in His own words.

I loved the day they asked Him, "Is it right to pay taxes to Caesar or not?" They were so confident He would indict Himself by speaking against Rome. Maintaining His composure, He simply asked for a Roman denarius. Holding the coin out to them He asked, "Whose portrait is this? And whose inscription?"

"Caesar's" they replied. Then He said, "Give to Caesar what is Caesar's and to God what is God's." You could've heard a pin drop in the crowd, it was so quiet.

I was so proud to be a part of His life.

But I could sense something was different that week. The parables He taught condemned the Jewish leaders. And I couldn't believe my ears the day He stood in the temple courts and denounced them.

"Woe to you scribes, Pharisees, hypocrites," He said. I

thought we'd all be killed when He called them a brood of vipers, children of hell, white sepulchres and blind guides. I've never been so glad to hear a sermon end as that one.

Then the unexpected happened.

As we shared the Passover meal, He did the strangest thing. He broke the bread and told us it was His body and that we should eat it. He took the third cup, the cup of blessing, and said it was His blood and that we were to drink it so that our sins might be forgiven. He spoke with such intensity that all of us were becoming a bit frightened so I jumped up from the table and told Him that I was ready to go with Him to prison and to death if necessary.

That broke the silence and everyone else chimed in as well and pledged Him their allegiance.

We thought He would drop the subject of dying at that point—but He didn't.

He turned to me—almost with tears in His eyes and said the most heartbreaking words ever spoken to me: "Peter, this very night you will betray me."

My heart felt as though it had been pierced through with a sword. I felt so hurt, so confused, and so embarrassed. "What did He mean by that?" I thought to myself.

After that, the events passed like runaway thoughts during a nightmare.

Judas left the room abruptly.

The Master took us to the Garden for prayer. I had never seen Him act that way before.

We tried to stay up and pray, but we kept falling asleep.

I was sound asleep, as were the others, when I was awakened by the noise of an angry crowd. Soldiers surrounded us with torches that lit the evening sky. My heart was pounding uncontrollably.

Then Judas stepped out from behind a soldier and went over to Jesus and kissed Him. At that, they seized Him. I grabbed a sword and swung at a soldier to protect Jesus. I only hit his ear. But Jesus touched him and healed the man. Then they carried Him off into the night.

A thousand questions rushed through my mind, "What does it all mean? What is happening?"

I can vaguely remember the remainder of events that transpired. But I'll never forget what happened to me as I sat by a fire in the courtyard near the house of the high priest where they had taken Him.

A servant girl noticed me in the firelight and said to the others that I was with Jesus. Without a thought, I said I never knew Him. Others joined in and accused me of being one of His closest friends. But I shouted all the louder that I'd never even seen the man, and I began to curse Him.

My curses were stopped by the crowing of a rooster in the distance.

Then I saw Him. He looked straight at me from across the courtyard.

I couldn't believe what I had done. I ran as hard as I could from the place, crying uncontrollably.

Thoughts of suicide filled my mind. There was no reason for life to go on for me—but something kept me from it.

Later, from a distance, I watched Him die on Golgotha's hill. For six long hours, His life's blood flowed from His veins onto the dusty ground beneath the cross. I died with Him that day.

The next three days were filled with confusion, loneliness and fear for us all. We locked ourselves in a room, afraid of what the Jewish leaders might do to us if they found us.

News came that His body had been stolen. John and I ran to the tomb to find out what had happened.

We found His grave empty—except for His burial

clothes. They were folded neatly on the place where He had lain.

When John and I went back to report to the group, some of the women had arrived saying He was alive, and they had seen Him and talked with Him.

We thought they were out of their minds, and we didn't hesitate to tell them so.

That is, until He appeared in the room with us. I don't mean that He came to the room and knocked on the door. He suddenly appeared right in the midst of the room where we were gathered—transcending time and space and matter.

I was filled with joy and shame at the same time. He spoke peace to us and stayed only a short time. Then He left.

Oh, how I wanted to speak to Him, but I was too ashamed of the way I denied Him. I knew He was disappointed in me. He could never trust me again.

A few days later, several of us went to the Sea of Galilee to fish. It was a beautiful morning. The gentle waves were brushing against the side of the boat and the gleaming of the morning sun on the water created a picturesque moment. We had fished all night but caught nothing. It didn't really matter though. My friends and I were together and that was enough.

Then we noticed the figure of a man we didn't recognize standing on the shoreline. He called out to us to cast our nets on the right side of the boat, assuring us that we would catch something. While I was thinking what a ridiculous suggestion that was, the others did as He had commanded. No one could believe what happened. The net was so heavy and full of fish we could hardly get it in the boat.

John looked at me and said, "It's the Lord!"

I panicked.

Like a child, I impulsively jumped into the water out of excitement and swam to shore.

When we arrived at the shore, He had breakfast waiting for us. While He talked with us, I just stared at Him, speechless. My mind replayed my denial of Him again and again. I could hear myself saying, "I don't know Him."

Then He fastened His eyes on me. I looked down at the ground.

After breakfast He asked me to take a walk with Him. Nervously, I did.

We walked a short distance from the others and He turned, looked at me and asked the strangest question: "Peter, do you love me?"

I was expecting Him to ask why I denied Him and cursed Him, but He never once mentioned it.

I was so caught off guard that I blurted out, "Yes, Lord. You know that I love You." Then He said to me, "Feed my lambs."

"What in the world did He mean by that?" I thought.

He asked the same question again, "Peter, do you love me?" What was He driving at? I replied, a little agitated, "Yes, Lord, You know that I love You." He said, "Take care of my sheep."

The third time He asked if I loved Him I was hurt. But the question forced me to honestly evaluate my love for Him.

I knew I loved Him. If I just had one more chance I would never deny Him again. So I said confidently, "Lord, You know all things; You know that I love You."

He smiled at me and said, "Feed my sheep." My heart was filled with joy because I knew He was giving me the second chance for which I longed.

And that's what I will do for the rest of my life—I will take care of His sheep.

The next time you face setbacks, bounce back with these timeless truths from the God of the second chance:

Failure is never final.
        Failure does not change our status with the Lord.
                Failure can be transformed into success.
        To fail is not to be a failure.
Failure does not disqualify us from service in the Kingdom.

Chapter 8

Answering God's Call

Since I am a minister, I am often asked at what point I first realized God was calling me into the ministry. My earliest awareness of God's call was when I was 8 years old. I did not grow up in a minister's home, so I had no idea what was involved in devoting one's life to pastoral ministry. But I knew, beyond a shadow of a doubt, God was calling me.

Later, when I was in high school and I was encouraged to think about my future career, all I could see myself doing was being a minister. When I was in college, the calling became inescapable, and I made a personal commitment to the call of God.

Celebrity caricaturist Ralph Barton, although successful and in high demand, took his own life in 1931. He left a note nearby that included these words, "I am fed up with inventing devices to fill up 24 hours of the day."

Ralph Barton failed to connect with the calling of God

and consequently fell prey to meaninglessness and emptiness. The thought of being called of God can be exhilarating or intimidating, depending on your perspective. Such a calling carries a deep sense of responsibility and requires humility.

Do you fear God might upset your plans if you start praying, "Not my will but Yours be done?" One of the most touching aspects of Jesus' ministry was the way He called people from all walks of life. The call of God cut across all ethnic, age, religious and gender lines. He called the great and the small, the educated and the uneducated, kings and princes, common men and statesmen, homemakers, entrepreneurs, politicians, tax accountants, rabbis and priests, the wealthy and the poor, Jews and Gentiles, women and children.

What would you think if I told you God has placed a calling on your life? I don't mean to imply you have to be a preacher or a missionary, but God *has* called you. How does that make you feel? Do you feel overjoyed, knowing your life has eternal significance? Or do you feel overwhelmed, doubting you will be able to live up to such a call? Do you fear God might upset your plans if you start praying, "Not my will but Yours be done?"

There are two sides to the coin of God's calling. On one hand, God calls every person into a relationship with Himself through Jesus. On the other hand, He has a specific purpose for every person. That doesn't mean your life is scripted—He has given us the freedom to make our own decisions. The call means we have a part to play in what God is doing in the world.

Marriage is a calling. Raising children is a calling. Every honorable profession is a calling. Financial giving is a calling. Service is a calling. Prayer is a calling. When we learn to hear and obey the call of God, we will face life with purpose and passion.

The calling of God occupies center stage in Scripture. Here are a few passages to consider:

- "My people, who are *called* by my name, will humble themselves and pray" (2 Chronicles 7:14).

- "Fear not, for . . . I have *called* you by name; you are mine" (Isaiah 43:1).

- "You also are among those who are called to belong to Jesus Christ . . . who are loved by God and *called* to be saints" (Romans 1:6, 7).

- "And we know that in all things God works for the good of those who love him, who have been *called* according to his purpose" (Romans 8:28).

- "And those he predestined, he also called; those he *called*, he also justified; those he justified, he also glorified" (Romans 8:30).

- "God's gifts and his *call* are irrevocable" (Romans 11:29).

- "God, who has *called* you into fellowship with his Son . . . is faithful" (1 Corinthians 1:9).

♦ "Live a life worthy of the *calling* you have received" (Ephesians 4:1).

♦ "Make your *calling* and election sure" (2 Peter 1:10).

Sometimes we don't hear the call of God clearly. We may think God is calling us when our emotions are playing tricks on us. A man was telling his neighbor, "I just bought a new hearing aid. It cost me $4,000, but it's state-of-the-art. It's perfect."

"Really?" answered the neighbor. "What kind is it?"

The man with the expensive hearing aid looked at his watch and said, "Twelve-thirty."

While we're on the subject of not hearing well: George, an 82-year-old man, went to the doctor to get a physical. A few days later, the doctor saw George walking down the street with a gorgeous young lady on his arm.

The doctor spoke to the man and said, "You're really doing great, aren't you?"

George replied, "Just doing what you said, Doc: 'Get a hot mamma and be cheerful.'"

The doctor said, "I didn't say that. I said you've got a heart murmur. Be careful!"

Getting On-line

The big question everybody's asking today is, Are you on-line? God has a distinct call for every person and we need to get connected on-line with God so we can know His will.

The apostle Paul heard the call on the Damascus Road and later wrote: "But when God, who set me apart from birth and called me by his grace, was pleased to reveal his Son in me . . . I did not consult any man" (Galatians 1:15, 16).

Paul tells us the calling of God is eter-

> God has a distinct call for every person and we need to get connected on-line with God so we can know His will.

nal. "He chose us in him before the creation of the world" (Ephesians 1:4).

God created us with a purpose and for a purpose.

For you created my inmost being; you knit me together in my mother's womb. I praise you because I am fearfully and wonderfully made; your works are wonderful, I know that full well. My frame was not hidden from you when I was made in the secret place. When I was woven together in the depths of the earth, your eyes saw my unformed body (embryo). All the days ordained for me were written in your book before one of them came to be (Psalm 139:13-16).

God ordained our lives even in the embryonic state. According to an article by Janet L. Hopson in the September/October 1998 issue of *Psychology Today,* "Behaviorally speaking there is little difference between a newborn baby and a 32-week-old fetus. A new wave of research suggests that the fetus can feel, dream, and even enjoy *The Cat in the Hat.* The abortion debate may never be the same."

The "book" of which the psalmist speaks refers to God's foreknowledge of and blessings on our lives at conception. "For we are God's workmanship, created in Christ Jesus to do good works, *which God prepared in advance for us to do* " (Ephesians 2:10, emphasis added).

As C.S. Lewis wrote, "There are no ordinary people."

Willpower

A billboard read, "There is no greater burden than a great opportunity." We are to walk "worthy of the calling" (Ephesians 4:1). Doing God's will is not always glitter and spotlights—in fact, it seldom is. The calling of God brings challenges and even criticism by others.

Moses discovered this truth soon after he led the Israelites out of Egypt and into the desert. The entire Book of Numbers centers around ten major complaints of the Israelites in the desert. The glory of Moses' call at the burning bush was soon replaced with the reality of leading people who didn't want to be led anywhere but back to Egypt where they were "comfortable."

> The calling of God brings us from the comfort zone to the cutting edge.

The calling of God brings us from the comfort zone to the cutting edge. Answering the call is a matter of continual obedience. We yield to the call instead of going our own way. It took Jonah a while to learn this lesson.

The call of God will be tested. The call of Jesus at His baptism was followed immediately by His testing in the desert by Satan, who sought to keep Jesus from His mission. It takes faith to answer God's call because it includes risk. Success is not always guaranteed, but here's the good news: When you fulfill your calling, you will know you are making a difference in the world. The call takes us outside ourselves so that we live for a higher purpose.

In his book, *And the Angels Were Silent*, Max Lucado offers the following challenge.[1]

1. Name the five wealthiest people in the world.

2. Name the last five Heisman Trophy winners.

3. Name the last five winners of the Miss America contest.

4. Name 10 people who have won the Nobel Prize.

5. Name the last half dozen Academy Award winners for Best Actor and Actress.

6. Name the last 10 World Series winners.

How did you do? The point is, no one remembers the headliners of yesterday. These are no second-rate achievers—they are the best in their fields. But the applause dies. Awards tarnish. Achievements are forgotten. Accolades and certificates are buried with their owners.

Here's another quiz:

1. List a few teachers who aided your journey through school.

2. Name three friends who have helped you through a difficult time.

---

3. Name five people who have taught you something worthwhile.

4. Think of a few people who have made you feel appreciated and special.

5. Think of five people you enjoy spending time with.

6. Name half a dozen heroes whose stories have inspired you.

Easier? The lesson is clear: The people who make a difference in your life are not the ones with the most credentials, the most money or the most awards. They are the ones who care.

The call of God requires a response. God's call is not forced on us—we have to surrender to His call. Jesus made this abundantly clear when He said, "Whosoever will . . ." (Mark 8:34). We must make a conscious choice to do God's will.

Jesus believed in willpower: "If anyone chooses to do God's will, he will find out whether my teaching comes from God or whether I speak on my own" (John 7:17). Toward the end of his ministry, Jesus "resolutely set out for Jerusalem" (Luke 9:51). Translated literally, He "set his face like a flint." We need the same level of determination to do God's will.

> God's call is not forced on us—we have to surrender to His call.

You see, it's not what we *feel*, it's what we *will* that makes the difference.

- Noah didn't *feel* like building an ark, but in holy fear, he built it to save his family.

- Abraham didn't *feel* like taking Isaac to Moriah, but he arose early in the morning and set out to the place where God showed him. On the mountain, he learned God provides if we trust Him.

- Moses didn't *feel* like going to Egypt and confronting Pharaoh, but he went in obedience to God's command and saw the power of God displayed.

- Caleb didn't *feel* like wandering 40 years in the desert, but he endured the hot sands of the Sinai in order to possess the Promised Land.

- Joshua didn't *feel* like accepting the challenge of leadership, but he found courage in the Lord and led the Hebrews into the Promised Land.

- Deborah didn't *feel* like leading Israel as a prophetess, but she took the challenge and guided the nation to victory in a time of war.

- David didn't *feel* like facing Goliath alone in battle, but he took his sling and five smooth stones and won the battle.

- Jeremiah didn't *feel* like being a prophet when he faced rejection and ridicule, but he was faithful to his calling.

◆ Shadrach, Meshach and Abednego didn't *feel* like facing the fiery furnace of Nebuchadnezzar, but they declared, "The God we serve is able to save us" (Daniel 3:17).

◆ Mary didn't *feel* like submitting to God's will and trying to explain a virgin birth to her fiancé, but she told the angel, "I am the Lord's servant" (Luke 1:38).

◆ Paul didn't *feel* like preaching at the cost of rejection, imprisonment and a martyr's death, but he could say, "I have kept the faith" (2 Timothy 4:7).

◆ Jesus didn't *feel* like going to the cross, but, for the joy set before Him, He endured the cross and obtained eternal redemption for humanity (Hebrews 12:2).

When Dr. Mihai Dimancescu was a resident at a Connecticut hospital, he made rounds one morning with the chief of neurosurgery. They came to a 24-year-old woman who had been in a coma for three months. "Don't waste time on her," the chief instructed. "She's never going to wake up."

A few weeks later, the woman regained consciousness. When Dimancescu asked if she could remember anything that happened while she was in the coma she said, "I remember that doctor saying I'd never get well. I made up my mind to show him here was a woman who had decided to fight for her life." Dimancescu says he's "seen it happen time and time again."[2]

Hey, God, Is That You?

How do we know when God is calling us? I have heard people say, "I know God is calling me to do something great, but I don't know what it is." That's illogical. When God calls, we will know His voice. He promises you "will hear a voice behind you, saying, 'This is the way; walk in it'" (Isaiah 30:21).

The call of God is definite and clear in the mind of the person who has been called. God is neither vague nor ambiguous, and His call is a clear trumpet sound requiring a prompt response of faith and obedience.

The call of God brings an inescapable sense of destiny and inner compulsion to do God's will. Jeremiah said, "But if I say, 'I will not mention him or speak any more in his name,' his word is in my heart like a burning fire, shut up in my bones. I am weary of holding it in; indeed, I cannot" (Jeremiah 20:9).

Jonah ran from the call of God only to find himself in the belly of a whale. He was then compelled to go to Nineveh. Both Jeremiah and Jonah tried to avoid God's will, but His call was inescapable.

When Jesus walked by the Sea of Galilee and called those fishermen, "*at once* they left their nets and followed him" (Matthew 4:20, emphasis added). Paul described this inner compulsion of God's call by telling the Ephesian elders, "Now, compelled by the Spirit, I am going to Jerusalem, not knowing what will happen to me there" (Acts 20:22).

Here are some practical ways you can know God's gifts and callings (Romans 11:29).

♦ *Interests*: What type of work and ministry are you interested in? Your gifts will follow your desires for ministry.

♦ *Fulfillment*: When you exercise your gifts and function in your calling, you will experience a sense of personal fulfillment. Does your current place of work and ministry bring you frustration, fear or fulfillment?

♦ *Confirmation*: Do other people confirm your gifts? Do they compliment you when you work and serve, telling you that you are in your niche? Remember, others will always recognize and confirm our gifts when we use them.

♦ *Productivity*: When we operate in our gifts, we will produce results for the kingdom of God. If, however, we are outside our gift and calling, we will be frustrated and fail to produce results.

♦ *Evaluation*: Honestly evaluate your strengths and weaknesses to discern whether or not you are using your gifts and serving where God wants you to serve.

♦ *Counsel*: What do the spiritual leaders and mentors in your life say about your gifts and callings? They, too, will confirm God's call on your life.

◆ *Recognition*: People in general often know when we are in the will of God. Evangelist Billy Graham was invited to preach in the Soviet Union long before Communism fell. Even the Communist government discerned Dr. Graham had God's message of hope for their nation. When people heard Jesus teach, they said, "He taught as one who had authority, and not as their teachers of the law" (Matthew 7:29).

When we connect with God's call we will experience enthusiasm for life. English clergyman Charles Kingsley wisely said, "We act as though comfort and luxury were the chief requirements of life, when all that we actually need to make us happy is something to be enthusiastic about."

One final point about the call of God: the calling keeps us focused. News commentator Dan Rather has a good way of keeping his professional objective always in his mind. He says he looks often at a question he's written on three slips of paper. He keeps one in his billfold, one in his pocket, and one on his newsdesk. The probing reminder asks, "Is what you are doing now helping the broadcast?"

The question for us is greater: "Is what you are doing now helping to advance the kingdom of God?"

Gethsemane Revisited

The Garden of Gethsemane is a beautiful olive orchard

outside Jerusalem. I have had the opportunity to visit it on several occasions. I like to find a place in Gethsemane to pray for a few minutes alone. I always feel compelled to pray the prayer Jesus offered in that Garden before He went to the Cross: "Father, if it is possible, may this cup be taken from me. Yet, not as I will, but as you will" (Matthew 26:39).

Gethsemane was a watershed event in Jesus' life. We also need a Gethsemane in our hearts where we can be alone with God and lay our lives before Him in full surrender to His will.

Of course, we should make plans and set goals—God wants us to do so. He created us with the capacity to dream, plan and achieve. But He wants us to do so in an attitude of complete surrender to His larger plan for our lives. When He breaks in and interrupts our plans to give us an assignment, we must respond by saying: "Speak, Lord, your servant is listening."

The Road Not Taken

As a high school senior in a literature class, I found myself deeply interested in the poetry of Robert Frost. His poem, "The Road Not Taken," made a strong impression on me:

> *Two roads diverged in a wood, and I —*
> *I took the one less traveled by,*
> *And that has made all the difference.*

Two roads are before us. The first is the road of the

will of the self—the path of self-determination. The second is the road of the will of God—the path that fills life with eternal purpose.

I have taken the road less traveled, the narrow path of the will of God, and I can truly say it has made all the difference. The road less traveled will make the difference for you as well. It is the pathway to repurposing your life.

Chapter 9

Bringing Out the Best in Others

I n his book, *The Double Win,* Denis Waitley challenges the law of the jungle seen in the competitive marketplace—win at all costs. People who live according to the law of the jungle climb the ladder of success and step over others on the way to the top—survival of the fittest. According to the law of the jungle, there must be a loser for every winner.

Waitley offers a new strategy over the old win-lose model. The "double win" concept says I can win and help you win at the same time. While I'm climbing the ladder of success, I will take you with me to the top. If I help you win, I also win.[1]

Jesus was the master of the double win. He taught people to dream. He imparted hope. He awakened the sleeping giant in those who followed Him.

Jesus brought out the best in others by imparting optimism—the disposition to look on the bright side of things. As His disciples, we are called to a place of leadership and influence. The main goal of leadership is to bring out the best in others by being agents of faith and optimism. The optimism of Jesus is clearly seen in Scripture: "If you believe, you will receive whatever you ask for in prayer" (Matthew 21:22).

> The main goal of leadership is to bring out the best in others by being agents of faith and optimism.

The Christian life is a plus, not a minus. It is a positive, not a negative. It is addition, not subtraction. It is multiplication, not division. Christ doesn't diminish you, He expands you. With Christ at the center of your life, all things are possible!

A third grader was making silly faces in the class and disturbing the other kids. The teacher came back to the boy in the back row, and said, "When I was a child, I was warned that if I made ugly faces and the wind changed direction, my face would freeze and stay like that forever."

The boy hardly blinked when he replied: "Well, Mrs. Smith, you can't say you weren't warned."

Future Tense Faith

Jesus' prayer in John 17, offered in the face of the Cross, exemplifies His faith in the future. The times in which Jesus lived were bleak. Rome ruled the world with an iron fist. The Jews in Jerusalem were oppressed. Cities were under military law. Taxes were exorbitant. People were depressed.

Then Jesus burst on the scene with a hope-filled announcement: "The kingdom of heaven is at hand" (Matthew 4:17, *NKJV*). The kingdom announcement meant God was breaking into history with a new work of grace and power. The day of liberty and peace was near.

How could Jesus have been so positive about the future? After His resurrection, He knew His followers would face persecution and hardship, but He saw life from God's vantage point. What did Jesus see while He was hanging on the cross, dying for our sins? Did He only see His executioners? Or the religious mob who mocked Him? Or the pain of His family and friends? No—He saw the salvation of the world. He saw you and me. "For the joy set before him he endured the cross" (Hebrews 12:2).

The fear factor of our time can be conquered by a Christ-centered optimism. Jesus prophesied of the last days:

> Men will faint from terror, apprehensive of what is coming on the world, for the heavenly bodies will be shaken. . . . When these things begin to take place, stand up and lift up your heads, because your redemption is drawing near (Luke 21:26, 28).

Adoniram Judson, missionary to Burma, understood optimism. He faced tremendous obstacles to his missionary endeavors, yet declared, "Our future is as bright as the promises of God."

In order to lead others and bring out the best in them,

we must give them a vision of hope for their lives and let them know they can make a difference in the world.

Believe in Them

I saw a billboard that read: "Do you believe in God? God believes in you." We talk a lot about our faith in God, but it would serve us well to make a Scriptural study of God's faith in us. After His resurrection, Jesus left His mission in the hands of 12 men and a larger group of disciples. They were to carry on His work in the world. Even

> We talk a lot about our faith in God, but it would serve us well to make a Scriptural study of God's faith in us.

though they failed Him when He went to the cross, He still believed in them.

How can we show faith in the people God has called us to lead?

1. *Look for hidden potential.* We are all diamonds in the rough. Jesus imparted a vision of greatness to His disciples and they lived up to it. I distinctly remember the significant people who saw my potential when I was young, although other people didn't see it. They helped shape my confidence.

Jesus said the kingdom of heaven is like a treasure hidden in a field that a merchant purchased for a large sum of money to possess the hidden treasure (Matthew 13:44). You and I are that hidden treasure. He gave His life on the cross to redeem us from sin so that the hidden treasure in all of us might be uncovered and put on display.

2. *Allow them to fail.* Each day is a new start. "His mercies begin afresh each day" (Lamentations 3:23, *NLT*). Travel light. Don't get bogged down with anxieties and failures. As Jesus said, "Do not worry about tomorrow, for tomorrow will worry about itself. Each day has enough trouble of its own" (Matthew 6:34).

3. *Think the best about others and expect the best from them.* Set high standards for those you lead. It shows your confidence in them. Dan Benson, in his book, *The Total Man,* says that for every positive word that most dads say to their children, they say 10 negative ones. They frequently use words like *don't* and *you can't* and *stop that* and *no.* But men aren't very good at positive words. Benson suggests that we could change our relationships with our children if we just learned to be positive.

4. *Speak the best about others.* "Love covers over a multitude of sins" (1 Peter 4:8). My mother was fond of the adage: "If you can't say something good about someone, don't say anything at all." We need to look for the good in others and always speak the best of them.

Two brothers were in the Mafia. One died, so his brother went to a priest and requested a Christian burial. The man promised the church a substantial financial gift if the priest would use the word *saint* in the eulogy for his brother. The priest agreed to preach the funeral. He knew the reputation of the two brothers and struggled to think of a way to incorporate the word *saint* in his remarks.

During the eulogy, the priest said to the congregation, "As you all know, the man before us was a low-down,

no-good scoundrel who lived a life of crime. But compared to his brother, he was a saint."

5. *Love again after you have been hurt.* Encourage
those you lead to carry on after they have failed. We
should bear with the failures of the weak and carry each
other's burdens (Romans 15:1; Galatians 6:2). If we
would truly mentor others, we must be there when they
fail to pick them up and prod them to keep pressing on.

Extraordinary Power in Ordinary People

Donna Lancaster was born without her lower legs or
knees, and, as an adult, reached a height of only 3 feet 10
inches. With the help of supportive parents, she learned
to walk, ride a bike, drive a car and fly an airplane. She
also graduated from college, held a variety of jobs and
married. As an adult, she uses artificial legs that make
her 5 feet 8 inches. She tells her story in her autobiography, *The Short and Tall of It: The Marvel of Our Existence
Is Incredible.*

We are made in the image of God. But there is a fly in
the ointment—the problem of sin. Sin keeps us from
reaching our spiritual potential. Sin marred the image of
God in us (see Psalm 51:4; Romans 3:23). Sin is missing
the mark. Sin is living a misdirected life—a life apart from
the plan and purpose of God. Jesus came to save us from
our sins and restore the image of God in us. "Therefore, if
anyone is in Christ, he is a new creation; the old has gone,
the new has come!" (2 Corinthians 5:17).

Jesus did not come simply to give the Sermon on the Mount, speak in parables, feed the multitudes, or walk on the water. He came to save us from our sins that we might be born again as sons and daughters of God. "You are to give him the name Jesus, because he will save his people from their sins" (Matthew 1:21).

Jesus awakens the greatness within and enables ordinary people to do extraordinary things. Everyone who met Jesus saw himself or herself in a new light. Take Peter for example. His name *Simon* means "a reed." But Jesus called

> Jesus awakens the greatness within and enables ordinary people to do extraordinary things.

him *Peter*, meaning "a rock." Think of it: from a reed to a rock! Peter was an ordinary person with extraordinary power—he was given the keys to the kingdom of heaven.

You are a new person with a new power. Repeat this vow of confidence: "He who is in [me] is greater than he who is in the world" (1 John 4:4).

Larger Than Life

Maturity is being larger than your adversities and smaller than your accomplishments. Jesus prayed for us: "My prayer is not that you take them out of the world, but that you protect them from the evil one" (John 17:15). The world can be a place of hostility for us, because the world system is hostile to God. "I have given them your word and the world has hated them" (v. 14).

Jesus knew His followers would face persecution and

many would die for their faith. Yet, in the face of such trials, the inner power of Christ enabled them to rise above their circumstances and become larger than life. The way of Christ is never the way of escape but of endurance.

Don't be discouraged when God chooses not to remove you from your adversity. He will bring you through. He makes a way when there seems to be no way. We look for a way out; He gives a way through! His power in you will enable you to handle everything you face with grace and with gratitude.

> Don't be discouraged when God doesn't remove you from your adversity. He will bring you through.

The deaths of the apostles, which are recorded in Foxe's *Book of Martyrs*, tell the story of a faith that is larger than life.

The first martyr of the church was Stephen, who was stoned in the streets of Jerusalem.

Matthew was killed by battle-ax in Ethiopia.

Mark died after being dragged through the streets of Alexandria during an idolatrous ceremony.

Luke was hanged from an olive tree by idolatrous priests in Greece.

Andrew was crucified in Edessa on an X-shaped cross.

Peter was crucified in Rome upside-down.

James the Great was beheaded in Jerusalem.

James the Less was beaten and stoned by the Jews at age 94.

Philip was scourged, thrown in prison and afterwards crucified in Phrygia.

Bartholomew was beaten, crucified and beheaded in India.

Thomas was run through with a spear by pagan priests in India.

Jude was crucified.

Simon the Zealot was crucified in Britain.

Matthias was stoned at Jerusalem and beheaded.

The apostle Paul was beheaded in Rome.

Of the Twelve, only John, the "beloved disciple," escaped a martyr's death.

Overcoming Obstacles . . . Achieving Our Goals

The disciples were commissioned to be Christ's witnesses to the ends of the earth, yet they would face incredible obstacles. So Jesus prayed for them and for us: "Protect them from the evil one" (John 17:15). Earlier he prayed, "Protect them by the power of your name" (v. 11). Evil is in the world in two forms: sin and suffering. We face the temptations of sin and the trials of suffering. No one is exempt. "The testing of your faith develops perseverance" (James 1:3).

Reaching your potential will be difficult. Your faith will be tested. Your convictions will be tempted. Your dreams will be challenged. Your good will be spoken of as evil. Your progress will be frustrated. Your hopes will be crushed. Your character will be questioned. Your name will be slandered. The question is, how will you respond?

Booker T. Washington used to carry schoolbooks for other children. As a slave, he was deprived of an education, although he longed to learn. Later in life he fulfilled his dream of receiving an education and became one of the most educated men of his day, founding the Tuskegee Institute in Alabama in 1881. Washington said, "Success is not measured by what one achieves in life, but rather by the obstacles one overcomes in the achievement of that success."

If you can accomplish your dream by your own power, your dream is not big enough. You need a dream

> If you can accomplish your dream by your own power, your dream is not big enough.

that keeps you on your knees in prayer, depending on God for His power—a dream that says, with man this is impossible but with God all things are possible (Matthew 19:26; Mark 10:27)!

Bringing out the best in others means teaching them how to handle life at its worst. Show them how to overcome their obstacles through faith as they achieve their goals.

We are to "spur one another on toward love and good deeds" (Hebrews 10:24). Philip Yancey tells the story of an African safari on which he saw a mother giraffe taking care of her newborn offspring. Shortly after the calf was born, she began to kick him, and it looked like she was intentionally hurting her baby. She did it again and again. Each time, the little giraffe would get up on his wobbly legs and try to walk. She continued kicking him. Finally, he quickly stood up and ran away from her.

Yancey turned to the guide and asked, "Why does the mother giraffe do that?" The guide answered, "The only defense the giraffe has is its ability to get up quickly and outrun its predator. If it can't do that, it will soon die." God often comes to our comfort zones where we are lying still and kicks us into action. We should do the same with the people we mentor.

Molding Character

Mentoring others is really about molding their character. Who a person *is* is more important than what a person *does*. Jesus prayed for us: "Sanctify them by the truth; your word is truth" (John 17:17).

We are living in an age of crisis of character. The root of the word *character* is the Greek word for "engraving." When applied to human nature, character is the enduring mark left on a person by life that sets him or her apart as an individual. The greatest power of all is the power of a good name that comes from a life of integrity.

The Greek word translated *sanctification* also means holiness. What does it mean to be sanctified? First, it means to be set apart for God's special use. Israel was set apart for God's work as "a kingdom of priests and a holy nation" (Exodus 19:6). Even the Corinthians were called "saints," and they had many spiritual problems.

To be sanctified also means we are equipped for the tasks God has assigned to us. God has "given us everything we need for life and godliness" (2 Peter 1:3). We are to teach people to face life masterfully.

Finally, to be sanctified means to be different, distinct, uncommon, special and unique. Jesus prayed, "They are not of the world any more than I am of the world" (John 17:14). In Scripture,

> To be sanctified means to be different, distinct, uncommon, special and unique.

the tithe is called holy because it is different from other money. The Temple is called holy because it is different from other buildings. The Bible is called holy because it is different from other books. The priests are called holy because they are different from other men. The Sabbath is called holy because it is different from other days. Israel is called holy because she is different from other nations. The church is called holy because it is different from other organizations. Likewise, Christians are called holy because they are different from other people.

God's work of holiness is progressive as He conforms us to the image of His Son. Who you are is the ultimate achievement—the person is more important than the performance. The ultimate goal of leadership is to bring out the best in others by molding their character into the image of Jesus.

Henry Ford was once asked, "Who is your best friend?"

He replied, "My best friend is the one who brings out the best in me."

Chapter 10

Discovering Your Destiny

Discovering Your Destiny

Former President Ronald Reagan once had an aunt who took him to a cobbler for a new pair of shoes. The cobbler asked young Reagan, "Do you want square toes or round toes?"

Unable to decide, Reagan didn't answer, so the cobbler gave him a few days. Several days later the cobbler saw young Reagan on the street and asked him again what kind of toes he wanted on his shoes. Reagan still couldn't decide, so the shoemaker replied, "Well, come by in a couple of days. Your shoes will be ready."

When the future President did so, he found one square-toed and one round-toed shoe! "This will teach you to never let people make decisions for you," the cobbler said to his indecisive customer.

"I learned right then and there," Reagan said later, "if you don't make your own decisions, someone else will."[1]

Quality of life is a matter of choice, not chance. We

hear a lot of talk today about destiny. Destiny does not mean God has predetermined every detail of life and we have to live in a panic-mode going to prophets or counselors to discover it. Destiny means God created us with unlimited potential. You and I determine our destiny by choosing to do God's will and by taking responsibility for our lives.

Ours is the day of the great cop-out. You know the story of Adam and Eve's disobedience. When God confronted them, they played the blame game. Adam blamed Eve. Eve blamed the serpent. And the serpent didn't have a leg to stand on! (You saw that one coming, didn't you?)

Social scientist Charles Sykes tells the story of an FBI agent who embezzled $2,000 and used it for gambling. When he was fired for his crime, the agent went to court and successfully argued that his gambling behavior was a handicap, protected under the Americans with Disabilities Act. The FBI was forced to reinstate him. It is classic case of victim psychology—what Sykes calls "selfist psychology."[2]

God comes to us, as He came to Adam and Eve in the Garden, and asks, "What have you done?" He doesn't ask, "What have others done to you?" He doesn't ask, "What privileges have you been denied?" He doesn't ask, "Were you raised in a dysfunctional family?" He doesn't ask, "Has society treated you unfairly?"

> It is only when we assume responsibility for our actions that we are made whole and can live effectively.

He asks, "What have *you* done?" It is only when we assume responsibility for our actions that we are made whole and can live abundantly. We are not responsible for what happens to us, but we are responsible for how we respond.

The Will of God

Our destinies are not predestined; they are determined every day by the choices we make. God created us with the freedom to choose—that is what separates us from animals, which act on instinct and conditioned behavior.

For many people, the will of God seems a lot like Winston Churchill's 1939 description of the action of Russia: "It is a riddle wrapped in a mystery inside an enigma."

Discovering God's will is somewhat like the mythical search for the Holy Grail. We believe it exists and search intently for it, but it always seems to be just beyond our grasp.

What is the will of God? The term *will of God* is used four different ways in Scripture.

First, the *sovereign will* of God means He reigns over creation and history, working out "everything in conformity with the purpose of his will" (Ephesians 1:11).

The *redemptive will* of God means He planned for our salvation through the atoning work of Jesus "before the creation of the world" (1 Peter 1:20).

The *moral will* of God means He created us to reflect

His moral and spiritual qualities. Morality still matters to God, even in our age of moral relativism. "It is God's will that you be holy" (1 Thessalonians 4:3). "In everything give thanks; for this is the will of God" (5:18, *NKJV*).

Finally, the *personal will* of God means He created every person with purpose. We all have a part to play in God's grace. If He knows when a sparrow falls to the ground and if He has numbered the hairs on our heads, as Jesus said, then we can rest

> Inside the will of God there is no failure and outside the will of God there is no success.

assured He knows everything about us, and He has a plan for our lives. I sincerely believe that inside the will of God there is no failure and outside the will of God there is no success.

Success is not measured by fame, fortune, power or pleasure; it is doing the will of God and surrendering our hearts to His purpose. Success is living the prayer of Jesus: "Not as I will, but as you will" (Matthew 26:39). Success is saying with Paul, "To me, to live is Christ and to die is gain" (Philippians 1:21). Success is being a "living sacrifice" and practicing God's "good, pleasing and perfect will" (Romans 12:1, 3).

A Special Relationship

Jesus modeled a special relationship with the Father in which He was fully submissive to the will of God. "'My food,' said Jesus, 'is to do the will of him who sent me and to finish his work'" (John 4:34). Again He said, "I seek not to please myself but him who sent me" (5:30).

God said of King David, "He will do everything I want him to do" (Acts 13:22). David prayed, "I delight to do Your will, O my God, and Your law is within my heart" (Psalm 40:8, *NKJV*).

Occasionally, people tell me, "I know God has something very special for me to do." He has something special for *all* of us.What God wants most is for us to walk closely with Him.

Quality of Life

The most important verse in the Bible about the will of God is Romans 8:29, "Those God foreknew he also predestined to be conformed to the likeness of his Son." God's will is for us to model our lives after the example of Jesus. God is more concerned with who we *are* than what we *do*. Paul says that being filled with the knowledge of God's will means we may "live a life worthy of the Lord and may please him in every way: bearing fruit in every good work, growing in the knowledge of God" (Colossians 1:10).

Are you living up to your potential? Are you walking worthy of the calling you have received? Are you practicing the will of God as you already know it? Is your greatest desire to please the Lord and bring glory to Him? Are you bearing spiritual fruit in your own life and in your witness? Is the world a better place because of your spiritual influence? Are you maturing in Christlikeness? Are you pressing on to know God more completely?

We need to move beyond *seeking* God's will to *doing* God's will; from *praying* about God's will to *practicing* God's will.

A Process, Not a Blueprint

God does not have a specific will for every decision we face. Most of the decisions we make can be made on the basis of common sense, counsel from others and guidance from Scripture. There is no script written for your life from before eternity. God's will has flexibility. Destiny is not predetermined. We have the power and privilege to make decisions. God only wants us to use our freedom to make choices that honor Him and benefit others. If our decisions meet those criteria, they will be sound.

> We need to move beyond *seeking* God's will to *doing* God's will; from *praying* about God's will to *practicing* God's will.

God promises us wisdom for making decisions. "If any of you lacks wisdom, he should ask God, who gives generously to all without finding fault, and it will be given to him" (James 1:5). God gave us brains and He expects us to use them. The will of God is general, and the wisdom of God is specific to individual choices. We, then, are to set goals and make plans, but do everything with a submissive heart to the will of God. "You ought to say, 'If it is the Lord's will, we will live and do this or that' " (4:15).

A wealthy man was critically ill. His doctor told him, "There's only one thing that will save your life—a brain transplant. It's experimental and very expensive."

"Money is not object," the man said. "Can you get a brain?"

"There are three available," replied the doctor. "The first was from a college professor, but it'll cost you $50,000."

"Don't worry, I can pay. What about the second?"

"It was a rocket scientist's and will cost $100,000."

"I've got the money. And I'd be a lot smarter too. What about the third?"

"The third was from a Washington, D.C. politician. It will cost you half a million dollars."

"Why so much for the politician's brain?" he asked.

"Because it's never been used." (My apologies to my politician friends.)

God Reserves the Right to Interrupt Our Plans

Make plans, set goals and dream dreams, but bring them all before God and pray, "Not my will, but Yours be done." At times God will interrupt our plans with a special, definite call to do something He desires us to do. God reserves the right to interrupt our plans with His calling. "Many are the plans in a man's heart, but it is the Lord's purpose that prevails" (Proverbs 19:21). Paul writes, "You are not your own, you were bought at a price" (1 Corinthians 6:19, 20).

This doesn't mean you need to quit your job next week and relocate to China or Africa or the 10/40 window. But it might mean the Lord wants you to volunteer to serve in the children's ministry, or take a short-term missions trip, or serve at a homeless shelter or youth detention center. Or, the will of God may even mean a major career change if God so directs.

> God reserves the right to interrupt our plans with His calling.

The most important thing is to be yielded. Remember the prayer I cited earlier: "I delight to do Your will, O my God, and Your law is within my heart" (Psalm 40:8, *NKJV*). What a liberating prayer! When you and I pray that prayer with sincerity, we will be free from the cares of this life and free to obey the call of God.

Here's an important point: It is God's responsibility to give us the call—we don't have to go looking for it. Let me offer some practical pointers for knowing God's will. Correlate your personal desires, spiritual gifts and natural abilities. What do you want to do with your life? What do you enjoy doing? The will of God, as far as your vocation, will match up with your talents, abilities and desires. But our desires need to be submitted to the lordship of Jesus. As Paul says, we are *living sacrifices* (Romans 12:1)!

One Step at a Time

Many people want to know the future, but God wants

us to walk by faith and trust Him with the future. He unfolds His plan for us little by little, one step at a time. God may give you a glance into something that will happen at a future time. If He does, treasure that revelation of His will in your heart. Wait for it, for God will surely bring it to pass.

Think of the call of Abraham. God called him to leave his home and go to the unfamiliar land of Canaan. He "obeyed and went, even though he did not know where he was going" (Hebrews 11:8). He knew the general direction, but had to take the first step and trust God to lead him the next step. "Those

> Life with God is an ever-unfolding adventure.

who are led by the Spirit of God are sons of God" (Romans 8:14). To be led by the Spirit means to fully surrender to God's will without necessarily knowing what His will is.

Surrendering to God is risky. He doesn't always show us what lies around the next corner, or the next year, or 10 years from now. Instead, He expects us to walk by faith and not by sight. Life with God is an ever-unfolding adventure.

In the movie, *Indiana Jones and the Last Crusade,* Indiana searches for the Holy Grail. His journey finally led him to the place where the Grail was hidden. He found himself standing on the ledge of a steep chasm, which he had to cross to retrieve the Grail. There appeared to be no way to cross. Gathering his courage, he decided to take a "leap of faith." As he stepped out onto what seemed to be nothing, his foot landed safely on a camouflaged bridge spanning the chasm.

That's faith: Stepping out onto nothing, because God says to, then finding that we have stepped onto His solid path for our lives!

When the wine of celebration was almost gone, Mary told the servants at the wedding in Cana, "Do whatever he tells you" (John 2:5). When they did as Jesus instructed, the water turned into wine!

Ordering Our Steps

David wrote Psalm 37 in his latter years. As an elderly man, he had endured life's changing seasons—ups and downs, triumphs and tragedies, joys and sorrows, accomplishments and disappointments. As he looked back over the course of his life, he could trace clearly the hand of God that had guided him every step of the way. "The steps of a good man are ordered by the Lord" (v. 23, *NKJV*).

God will direct our steps. Here are His promises to you:

- "He guides me in paths of righteousness for his name's sake" (Psalm 23:3).

- "He guides the humble in what is right and teaches them his way" (Psalm 25:9).

- "For this God is our God for ever and ever; he will be our guide even to the end" (Psalm 48:14).

⬥ "He shall direct your paths" (Proverbs 3:6, *NKJV*).

⬥ "I will lead the blind by ways they have not
known, along unfamiliar paths I will guide them; I
will turn the darkness into light before them and
make the rough places smooth. These are the
things I will do; I will not forsake them" (Isaiah
42:16).

⬥ "To shine on those living in darkness and in the
shadow of death, to guide our feet into the path of
peace" (Luke 1:79).

⬥ "When . . . the Spirit of truth, comes, he will guide
you into all truth" (John 16:13).

Through Many Dangers, Toils and Snares

Here's a popular myth: God only allows us to have
pleasant, easy experiences. Such is the American "feel
good" mythology. I'm not suggesting God will intentionally make life miserable—we do well enough at that.
But God will use times of testing to refine our character
and mold our personality so we are prepared for what He
has in store for us.

After the exodus from Egypt, God would not lead the
Israelites through Philistine country, although it was a
shorter route. Instead, He led them down to the Red Sea.
Why? Because God said, "If they face war, they might
change their minds and return to Egypt" (Exodus 13:17).
Although they left Egypt armed for battle, they weren't

ready for battle. Instead, He intended that they face the Red Sea and see His great power displayed on their behalf so they might learn to trust Him in the desert and

Embracing God's purpose begins with preparation.

one day be prepared to possess the Promised Land.

Embracing God's purpose begins with preparation. The 40 years the Hebrews spent in the Sinai desert were used by God to prepare them for the promises.

> Remember how the Lord your God led you all the way in the desert these forty years, to humble you and to test you in order to know what was in your heart, whether or not you would keep his commands (Deuteronomy 8:2).

When God orders our steps, He doesn't waste any time or life experience. He is always preparing us for what lies ahead. He sees the end from the beginning. He does all things well. "In all things God works for the good of those who love him" (Romans 8:28).

- There's no crown without a cross.

- There's no gold without the refiner's fire.

- There's no diamond without the stonecutter's tool.

- There's no reward without finishing the race.

- There's no harvest without planting.

- There's no victory without a battle.

- There's no mountain peak without a valley.

◆ There's no vessel without the potter's wheel.

A man found an emperor moth's cocoon and took it home to watch the moth emerge. One day, a small opening appeared in the cocoon and, for several hours, the moth struggled to get out, but couldn't seem to push its body past a certain point. The man decided something was wrong.

So he took a pair of scissors and cut an opening in the cocoon, allowing the moth to emerge easily. But its body was swollen and the wings were small and shriveled. He thought in a few hours the wings would spread out in their amazing beauty, but they didn't. Instead of flying freely, the moth dragged its swollen body and shriveled wings around.

The struggle necessary for the moth to pass through the cocoon is God's way of forcing fluid from the body into the wings for their full development. The man's intervention did nothing but maim the moth.

> Sometimes our struggle is exactly how God intends us to grow. Don't waste your sorrows.

Sometimes our struggle is exactly how God intends us to grow. Don't waste your sorrows. "Trust in the Lord with all your heart and lean not on your own understanding" (Proverbs 3:5).

God Always Has a "Plan B"

The lowest point in David's life was his affair with Bathsheba. Could he rebound from that? While his sin carried severe and long-lasting consequences, God led him out of his shame into a new season of life. "Create in me a pure heart," he prayed, "and renew a steadfast spirit within me" (Psalm 51:10).

Have you fallen short of God's plan or stumbled morally? Have you failed to answer God's call?

I spoke with a man who told me he missed the call of God on his life when he was young. He started seminary training for the ministry, but then got distracted and went into business for himself. Although he had a successful career, he felt as though something were missing. I told him God always has a "Plan B." I couldn't say whether he missed the will of God or not—the key issue was for him to use the rest of his years to serve the Lord.

God is the God of new beginnings. You, too, can have a fresh start! That's how you repurpose your life.

Endnotes

Chapter 3

[1] Howard Bean, "Higher Education," *Companions*, Nov. 2000.

Chapter 4

[1] Jack Canfield, Mark Victor Hansen, and Kimberly Kirberger, *Chicken Soup for the Teenage Soul* (Deerfield Beach, FL: Health Communications, 1997).

[2] Jamie Buckingham, *Power for Living* (West Palm Beach, FL: Arthur S. DeMoss Foundation, 1998), 44-45.

Chapter 5

[1] Carol Mann, *The 19th Hole: Favorite Golf Stories* (Longmeadow, MA: Borders Press, 1992).

[2] Bill Hybels, *Too Busy Not to Pray* (Downers Grove, IL: Intervarsity, 1998).

Chapter 8

[1] Max Lucado, *And the Angels Were Silent*, (Portland, OR: Multnomah, 1999).

[2] "Your Attitude Can Make You Well," *Reader's Digest*, March 1992: 73.

Chapter 9

[1] Denis Waitley, *The Double Win* (Old Tappan, NJ: Revell, 1985).

Chapter 10

[1] "Today in the Word," (Chicago: Moody Press, Aug. 1991) 16.

[2] Charles Colson, *Breakpoint*, Aug. 23, 2002.